AF632579

6 Habits for Relationship Success

A Western Experience for a Modern Indian Society

Geoff Herridge

PEACOCK BOOKS

Published by
PEACOCK BOOKS
B-2, Vishal Enclave, New Delhi-110 027
Phones : 2541 3460, 2542 9987, 2546 6842

Distributed by
ATLANTIC PUBLISHERS AND DISTRIBUTORS (P) LTD.
7/22, Ansari Road, Darya Ganj, New Delhi-110 002
Phones : 2327 3880, 2327 5880, 2328 0451
Fax : +91-11-2328 5873
E-mail : info@atlanticbooks.com
Web : www.atlanticbooks.com

Branch Office
5, Nallathambi Street, Wallajah Road,
Chennai-600 002
Phones : +91-44-6461 1085, 3241 3319
E-mail : chennai@atlanticbooks.com

Peacock Books is an imprint of
Atlantic Publishers and Distributors (P) Ltd.

Copyright © The Author, 2008

All rights reserved. No part of this publication may be reproduced, stored in a retrieval system, transmitted or utilized in any form or by any means, electronic, mechanical, photocopying, recording or otherwise, without the prior permission of the copyright owner. Application for such permission should be addressed to the publisher.

Printed in India at Nice Printing Press, Delhi

DEDICATION

This book is dedicated to my lovely wife, Wendy, and our three great children – Daniel, Matthew and Charlotte

Preface

I started to write this book by accident. I was undertaking some research on a current book that I am writing on my personal experiences with fitness and health and came across some books on relationships. I read some of these books and thought that perhaps I could write about my own experiences down.

I began to think about the things that really matter in my relationship and through this process I came up with six habits or characteristics that are important in my relationship. I wrote these down and then expanded each habit using further research, my own ideas and experiences, and my friend's and colleague's relationships to complete the book.

I showed the book to friends and was greeted with the comment 'is it this easy to have and maintain a great relationship'. I began to think that maybe I have a new and unique approach to the way people can conduct their own personal relationships.

I then happened to come across an article about the changes in India's economic and social environment. Like other countries such as China, India has been undergoing some enormous changes over the past twenty to thirty years. These changes will invariably affect the way people live, work and play. Personal relationships are therefore also affected and these changes can cause some real problems if people are not ready for them. Traditional ways of courtship and marriage often do not meet the needs of people in a more modern society. People have started avoiding marriage as desires to rise economically and professionally have taken precedence over relationships. They are finding it difficult to sustain their marital relations, and the cases of divorce and separation are on the increase.

I studied and researched India's changes and believed that what I had written could equally apply to the people of that country. After all, many Indians have started to adopt the behaviours and characteristics found in the Western world—for better and for worse.

By using the information in this book I hope the readers will gain a better understanding of relationship behaviour. We all want the best out of our life with someone who we care deeply about. We all make mistakes and we can learn from them. Having the basic knowledge of what will make a relationship work will help us along the path to a more fulfilling life.

GEOFF HERRIDGE

Contents

Introduction

Habits

Habits are patterns of behaviour that allow us to perform many of our daily tasks without thinking about it, such as cleaning our teeth. They are also tasks, movements, thoughts or actions that make us feel good and can be good or bad. These processes start out as childhood routines and they continue throughout our lives. Habits take up our lives and control our behaviour to a large extent. In a lot of cases we would not get things done if we did not have habits to rely on. They get us out of bed at the same time each morning so we have time to get to work. I have my daily habits (or routine) that I usually undertake at the same time so that I know how I am going—at other times I enjoy moving out of the habits I have I may have just for a change. Holidays and even just weekends can provide that great break that helps to refresh us. The habits are often a routine we follow.

Habits are patterns of behaviour that we undertake at a particular time and this type of behaviour is repeated to either make us feel good or so that we do not feel so bad. We have all had or still have bad habits (such as smoking or drinking) and these are often the hardest to give up even if the desire to stop is there—the will or discipline is usually the biggest hurdle and the 'want to' has to be strong enough. We all know of friends who have tried to give up a bad habit but have failed at numerous attempts. At times there will be that physical and emotional addiction that makes bad habit breaking difficult.

People generally want to move away from any pain or unhappiness and will often take up bad habits such as alcohol or drugs to try and block out these experiences. However, these habits will more often than not make them feel worse.

We need to look at our various habits, assess them and decide if we can improve on them.

Why this Book?

In observing and listening to others I have also looked at my own, and what I consider successful, relationship with my wife, Wendy, of 21 years and partner of 26, and I'd like to take you on some of our journey. People have asked whether I am an expert in relationships or an expert in Indian society. I am neither, but then most of us are not experts in anything. We all have stories and experiences to tell, and some of us are willing to share these stories with others. In reading these experiences we take bits and pieces and apply them to our own lives. I have outlined what I believe works in an intimate relationship, but of course there will be other experiences out there that are different.

I believe many relationships are not functioning the way many people intended them to when they first entered them. These observations are often of first hand experiences from acquaintances and friends, research, and advice from others. I read about and have seen relationships in countries such as India where society is going through major changes that affect the people in that country. Sometimes, the people in that country start to come into contact with influences from the West, which can have its good and bad points. Relationships in India have changed greatly over the past ten to twenty years—there have been some very positive changes and changes that are not so good.

This book was originally written for readers in the West as the issues and points I am making relate to a 'Western style' relationship. However, with the change happening in India, I believe I can also offer the Indian people some ideas that they may be able to use in their own relationship as these changes do happen. As people of nations such as India come into contact with different cultures and like what they see, they will start to adopt many of these new things. And there will always be that initial struggle as there is that adjustment period as the two cultures clash—there will often be the older generation that lives with the traditional culture and the younger people who embrace the changes but still have respect for their parents and grandparents who perhaps may not accept new ways of thinking and doing things.

Studies and research of what are good and bad relationships have been conducted in the West for many years and there are many good ideas for making relationships work. I hope what is in this book will help put your, the reader, on the way to a great and happy relationship.

Both in India and the West, women are more likely to end a relationship than a man, which suggests that men's understanding of what women want or need from a relationship is perhaps not clear. While I am critical in this book of the way men do approach relationships, I do so in the hope that improvements can be made—it is not possible to make improvements without knowing where these improvements should be made and I believe we are all open to new ideas. However, this book is very much for both men and women.

What this book is trying to achieve is to identify a number of good habits that 'practised' on a regular basis will become part of our lifestyle. Undertaken over a period of time they become second nature and require little thought. They do not require a great deal of thinking. If you can see that these habits have an important purpose then it will make it easier to use them.

Chapters 1 and 2 in this book relating to Relationship Change in India and Choosing Your Partner are not one of the habits—I have included them as background on what changes have been occurring in India and some ideas for those who are looking for a partner or who are in a relationship that is still new and are looking for guidance. The habits I propose begin with Chapter 3—Understanding Your Partner and Your Relationship.

I like a successful, happy marriage or relationship to undertaking a job (or career) that one enjoys—perhaps something that we have a passion for. Not many of us are fortunate enough to be in this situation, but if our motivation to do a good job is always high, we seem to have the energy to achieve anything and we are good and successful at it. A boring job often means we do not like the organization one is working for and the actual job itself, and our self-esteem often suffers.

Relationships are similar. Sadly many people put more effort into their job or career than a relationship with their partner, by working long hours or spending more time with their work colleagues. A job or career can be more easily changed—relationships, once in trouble, are more difficult to repair and cause more unhappiness.

How to Get the Best Use out of this Book?

The next few chapters will help to provide some structure and discipline in our relationship, while allowing flexibility as circumstances change. But rather than follow any general model that can be fitted to all relationships, I think it is important that we each focus on our own circumstances—our past and present—to find solutions to relationship success. Therefore, not everything in this book applies to our own relationship. Yes there are some common principles that will be right for most relationships such as good communication and understanding your own partner, however, I am hoping that you will think about where your relationship is and develop your own path to success using some of the guidance in this book.

Changing what we do is the key to changes that you want to bring into your relationship. In most cases we can only do what is in our control and we respect that our partner has his/her own needs. By trying to control our partner we end up frustrated. While we cannot make our partner talk to us, we can take the initiative and talk to them or have a relationship that encourages communication.

The guidance provided in this book is not meant to imply that we give ourselves to our partner all the time—we can and should be eager to please our partner without being too subservient. A giving relationship will provide far more pleasure than one that one partner receives all the time.

If you can identify and act upon our partner's needs, desires and wants (provided they're reasonable) then we're indicating that our relationship is important. Our partner will hopefully respond to the changes that we are bringing into the relationship, with the result that we will both become more involved in the relationship and bring new meaning to it.

We sometimes see geese flying in a V-formation—there could be over thirty in such a flock. It is estimated that the geese can achieve an improvement of up to 70% by flying in this formation through more uplift. As the lead bird gets tired it moves towards the rear to allow another bird to take over the front position. While flying they're constantly communicating, offering each other encouragement. If a bird becomes injured or for whatever reason flies or drops to the ground a couple of other birds may follow this sick one and remain with it until it dies or can fly off again. Sometimes, they will re-join the flock or set out on their own, establishing a new formation. These birds care for and encourage each other, draw strength from one other and move forward more efficiently through their combined actions. We can learn from this pretty simple behaviour. Our relationship can be seen as a partnership in which we work together by communicating to find common goals, looking for efficiencies, and identifying, and drawing from, each other's strengths. There will also be times when we need to stop and take care of our partner.

Some relationships are beyond help and are better ended—they can be very hurtful to both partners, particularly if there is violence, and to any children involved. However, if we can start thinking about where our relationship is at the moment and how it can be improved using some of the thoughts in this book, we can improve our relationships. We need to be honest with ourselves. It may take time but if the effort and consistency is there the rewards will follow. Changes can be undertaken in stages or slowly so as not to be so difficult. After a period we will find that our actions in the relationship will become second nature. These changes will also help us as an individual and will help us in all walks of life as we become more confident in things around you.

Some of the suggestions in this book require more repetition than others for them to become a habit. For example, achieving a good level of fitness and health will take time, motivation and discipline. A greater understanding of our partner will require some thinking, and improved communication requires an effort and practice. Actions repeated over and over will enable habits to form, which will then become part of our lifestyle—if we are serious about improvements this is where we want to be. And we need to get rid of old habits that are not the same as our values.

In our relationship we can examine any reasons why our present behaviour is leading to bad habits (for example, a 'need' to criticise or judge our partner perhaps as a means for helping our own low self esteem; a habit which leads to tension and conflict) and use this to move towards a new behaviour in which we praise and encourage our partner. Our partner will feel good, and we will be able to influence their feelings in a positive way which will affect the way we feel about ourselves. We have now achieved two good outcomes rather than two bad ones and this change will encourage us to continue. We need to listen to these feelings as I assume we all want the best outcome in our relationship.

A common thought in the habits is communication, particularly with respect to listening. It is generally an area that requires the most effort and understanding in a relationship but if it is not good it can cause the most damage. Communication, and conversation, is important to a relationship as it is a way of showing that we and our partner are interested in each other. This book also focuses on valuing ourselves and the importance of self-respect. A happy relationship will involve partners who believe in themselves and are confident with each other. This book also looks at ways to improve ourselves so that we can bring new ideas to our relationship as well as help to freshen it.

Looking at ourselves and our relationship is not easy. We may end up not liking what we see as we pick up on every fault, or we may fear to act just in case we get something wrong. We need to try and get the balance right and it will be important for improvement and progress in our relationship.

Our moods, how angry we get and how often we smile or frown will be picked up by our partner and will often affect the way they feel. We smile at people as we walk down the street and if we get a smile back we feel good. If we don't, we ask ourselves 'what is the matter with them...' and our thoughts become negative. We need to be aware then how our mood influences how our partner feels—we can look at some of the ideas in this book and see how they may not just affect ourselves, but also our partner.

In looking for improvements through positive thinking, we can look to see where we want to go in our life, but we do this by looking at how we can change anything in the present moment—if we are to enjoy life we must live and create things at this moment rather than in the future as the future does not exist. We also learn from what our experiences have been in the past but we don't look at them too much as those experiences have passed. We will be more successful at achieving our goals if we move towards an outcome that we would like to achieve, rather than away from our current state. For example, we may not be the world's greatest communicator, or the fittest person alive. That may be where we are at the moment. Looking at becoming a better talker or a healthier person, rather than the fact that we may be over-weight or have difficulty raising or discussing issues is more important. This way we are able to be positive rather than negative.

I'll read a good book quickly and the other night Wendy asked me how I enjoyed the book I had just finished, and remarked how quickly I had read it. She asked whether I just read the words quickly or take the time to picture what I am reading. I imagine each scene and have a picture in my head of each person and place in the book. My images will be different to the next person's. When reading the words in this book, we need to take the time to develop pictures or images of what is being described or suggested. It may be how our partner talks to us or other people, an image of ourselves agreeing with our partner, talking with them, helping them with a task or perhaps going to watch or participating in one of their interests.

We can picture ourselves undertaking the fitness and health program described and imagine the results. I have included some basic ideas on physical and emotional intimacy. Thinking about our partner and picturing ways of improving our level of intimacy from the simple holding of hands or more cuddles to a more intimate and emotionally rewarding love making makes the action easier. We all have an imagination and enjoy day dreaming at times. We should put it to good use.

We need to try it out different things in our life and discover whether it works for us otherwise the words in this book will mean nothing. No one can undertake the habits in the book for us; it is our individual responsibility and action that will make any changes happen. This book has provided us with some ideas that we can use or adapt to our own circumstances. The question we need to ask ourselves then is what we will do with these ideas.

Relationship Change in India

1

There have been some major transformations in Indian society over the past twenty to thirty years. The major change, of course, has been the economic growth that the country has experienced in this time. With this change have come enormous opportunities for the local people to experience a higher standard of living, an opportunity to earn large amounts of money, and the chances to experience more in life than say their parents or grandparents. The uptake of Western culture has also meant some large transformations in relationships and marriage. These influences can be both positive and negative, and because the world has become such a smaller place due to globalization, it is very difficult for most societies to avoid outside influences. Every culture has something good to offer and I believe it is a case of having a balance between cultures—draw out the good and try and dispense with the bad. I have outlined below what I understand are some of the major changes that have been occurring in India:

1. Western education has made the Indian people more liberated as far as marriage is concerned. Younger people want to study further, obtain a job and start a career before they marry. The age when people marry has also increased over the years.

2. Traditional extended families, which have provided the support are giving way to the nuclear family, which means that assistance in the household by the in-laws or grandparents is not as common.

3. Parents are becoming more educated about the effects of girls becoming married at too young an age. Early marriage can

prevent girls from gaining a good education that is needed for personal development, preparation for adulthood and to assist them in their family life. Studies indicate that an average woman with several or more years of education will marry four years later than someone with little education, and will have 2-3 fewer children. Little education means missing out on socializing skills, including making friends outside the family circle. It also means that there is less chance of developing independence.

Those women who are abandoned, divorced or widowed have no skills to earn their living and may pushed into exploitative professions. There is a greater chance of joining or staying within the ranks of the poor—early marriage can therefore contribute to a life of poverty and a lack of independence.

4. Indian culture is becoming more and more under the influences from the West. Internet access, mobile phones and Western television shows are now freely available and have improved communication between people which has also influenced the way people seek partners.

5. In rural communities particularly, pre-puberty marriage for girls was the rule. In the late twentieth century, the age of marriage has risen in villages, almost to the levels that is seen in cities. Laws governing minimum marriage ages have been passed in various forms over the past decades, although such laws have not often had a great effect on actual marriage practices.

6. More women and men are working and studying together, in both urban and rural areas. There is a mixing of cultures and a greater choice of marriage partner is becoming very common. The rapid modernisation of the Indian cities and the influence of the West on the Indian media has also increased the speed of these changes.

7. Many young people have a better idea of what they want in life and who they want to live it with. Parents are now more inclined to support then in their decisions as in some cases the children will move away if the parents oppose what their

children want. As modernisation takes hold, the parents will often identify with what their children want.

8. Some Indians are now moving away from the traditional types of marriage arrangements such as arranged marriages, the dowry and marrying within the same caste or religion. Indians have realised that the arranged marriage has had its problems. It originated when child marriage was the custom in India. This marriage often occurred before puberty and prevented the children from marrying outside their caste or lower class for marriage. In many cases, it was not based on any spiritual value. A marriage such as this often meant that the woman became submissive to the husband and this was often reinforced through violence and abuse. In some cases, classified advertisements in newspapers or the use of marriage brokers are used when the family finds it difficult to find a suitable partner.

This is unlike modern marriage in which the relationship is based on mutual attraction, common interests and respect for each other. No amount of persuasion from the parents to marry someone they believe is suitable for them can make up for these factors.

9. Marriage in earlier times was stable, but sometimes the quality was low as a result of people having to marry someone chosen for them—it was something that people did not think about. It was not that people did not consider divorce; it was more like people felt shame over it. Divorce tended to affect women more, and they found it difficult to marry again once divorced. Now in modern India there are higher expectations from marriage and when a marriage is in trouble it is often the women who will look for professional counselling—they see themselves as the instigator for resolving conflicts and when this fails it often means the marriage is finished.

While the changing attitude in India seems to indicate that Indians feel that one should have the right to divorce, it can still have a stigma attached to it. There continues to be sections of Indian society that feel divorce is never an option, regardless of how abusive the relationship is or incompatible the partners are. A divorced woman often will return to her family, but may not be all that welcome.

10. Marriage is very much in a transitional phase in India and there is more emphasis on equality between males and females. However, this has not always come with changing attitudes such as accepting each other's strengths and weaknesses and accepting division of labour within the household. As a result, the divorce rate in India has increased dramatically over the past few years. As a Court advocate mentions:

> Until 1988 only one civil court handled divorces under the Hindu Marriage Act. Today three family courts are working long hours to deal with petitions from all religious groups. It is assumed then that the divorce rate has greatly increased. Even women from the lower strata file for divorce these days. Women were more accepting two decades ago of chinna veedu.

What has also happened has been the high divorce rate between those who have been married for 15-20 years, where divorces are now occurring because of the husband (in many cases) having an affair or there is violence in the marriage. Marriage counsellors are now becoming more important as a means for trying to save marriages particularly if marriages in India become easier to obtain and are more acceptable.

Like in the West, marriage in India is strongly institutionalised and there is generally a strong desire on behalf of partners to try and save them and to build a stable relationship.

11. The newly found freedom has resulted in a more openness about sexual behaviour. Traditionally, sexual matters tended to be hidden or suppressed according to the social norms found in the joint family system, or cultural and religious factors. The general lifestyles of the people, and this includes sexual behaviour has often been governed by these practises and can still have a powerful influence. More individualistic thought and greater exposure to books, magazines and movies have allowed sexual expression to become more open and people more inquisitive.

12. The individualism and greater self-interest, which often characterises what happens in the West, is suited to a society that encourages people to work and perform to their potential

and to be more like entrepreneurs in their business dealings. These changes and greater freedom have given people an opportunity and the flexibility to have relationships that perhaps have a greater chance to be happier—to take advantage of this requires work as people will not accept second best and are less likely to accept the standards and conditions of the older society.

13. While Indian people are increasingly being able to afford a car, a house and better jobs, there is more to life than just economic success—relationships between people are often seen as the key to happiness and this is increasingly being recognised.

14. Where there are these significant changes in the economic and social fabric of a society there will always be upheavals, and impacts felt at the individual level and within relationships are often the first to feel that change, for better or worse. With economic growth comes both fears and hopes. As society becomes more open adjustments are required—behavioural changes are bound to follow. While then Indian people are now more caring about their family life and personal values, divorce is now seen as a reasonable alternative to an unhappy marriage. A newspaper editor in Mumbai stated:

> One of the several causes of the divorce rate is the influx of books and movies from the West. Perhaps people thought that capitalism is okay, so then it may also be okay to have affairs like they have in the West where more freedom in relationships has led to higher rates of affairs and divorces.

Women in India are beginning to have more economic independence, so that they are able to exert more influence within a relationship and divorce is a more viable option if a marriage is unhappy as they have this increased financial independence. They are able to have more general decision-making power as well as issues concerning money matters so that major domestic affairs are decided on a mutual basis, rather than by the male of the household. This reflects a more democratic process within the marriage, and is a sign of an equal and satisfying relationship.

Women's personal rights and dignity are preserved in this type of relationship. When women do consider divorce, one of the main factors in influencing them whether to take action is whether they can afford to be on their own. In a more capitalist society there are greater expectations to have a comfortable lifestyle and this can disappear through divorce as money and houses have to be divided. Also it is assumed that the couples will not consider divorce that lightly where there are children involved. They would rather keep the whole family together for the sake of the children, rather than choosing divorce. You will often see parents stay together until the children have grown up—however, research has shown that children are more likely to be happy where the parents are divorced but the family is happier, than a family that has parents together who fight all the time.

15. Women in India have traditionally undertaken most of the household chores, particularly as many of them were at home full time. However, with India's economic success this is now slowly changing, with husbands sharing more of the tasks as women are also in the workforce. Labour saving devices has also meant that the time spent doing housework has reduced to a level similar to the West.

16. As more young people nowadays consider their own personal development there is the concern that there may be less time spent on their marriages. Children always represent a large part of a marriage and the more children there are the more stress there is in a marriage. Consumerism and instant gratification now play a major role in people's lives.

In addition as India continues to develop into an economic superpower the people will face practical issues such as housing problems, migration from the countryside to cities, and unemployment. All of these will have an impact on their choice in partner. Many couples, and not those just in India, may now commit to marriage for the wrong reasons, particularly where traditional marriages start to become less common. For example, marrying someone with money is seen as one way of escaping poverty and setting up a secure financial future or there may be short-term employment prospects by marrying someone who works in a good company. In other cases, people may enter marriage because they feel that they are getting older and their prospects of marrying may disappear or be reduced by their age as well as their prospects to have children. Perhaps all their peers are getting married as well as pressure from parents. All these reasons can influence people to make a hasty decision, which they then regret. I touch on these issues in the next chapter.

17. With a stronger sense of independence among women the focus is now on the quality of a marriage. The husband can, of course, be intimidated by the new freedoms shown by the women in Indian society and how it is reflected in relationships. In some cases, the men are brought up thinking that women will conform to the belief that men are the most important factor in their lives. If this type of attitude is taken into a modern marriage it can cause problems.

18. That marriage is the best lifestyle to strive for is held by most people. Marriage is still seen as a life goal and something most people would like. There may, of course, be women who wish to live the single life. They may choose to remain single as they do not want to spoil their current lifestyle (which may include travel, spending money on clothes and not having children) by getting married.

Those women who favour the single life are on the increase, but still they are a small minority and confined to the cities. It is assumed that the priorities of Indian women will change after getting married, with their original priorities of spending on travel and clothes and not having children changing, as they grow into the marriage.

19. With the increased focus on love and money there is pressure, particularly on the men, to improve the family's financial situation. With the pressure at work to perform, to be a good provider at home, and to help to meet the needs of a more modern women (their more complex or higher standard of emotional needs, for example), men's role in Indian society has perhaps become more complex than in the past.

20. Following the trend set by celebrities people, particularly the middle class, are choosing to live together before they marry. The advantages of this have included the wish to see if each is compatible with the other and wanting to save money so that they can buy a house. It is not considered such a bad thing to do and not so frowned upon by the family as much. This type of arrangement has its problems, particularly if it is a new trend—for example, who has custody of the children if there is a break-up and what are rights of the women concerning property and maintenance.

As relationship change in India there will be mistakes made in relationships. It is natural that marriage and relationships will go through changes and adjustments. As more Western style characteristics become common within these relationships, people will recognize that marriage is a very important part of their lives and something that requires work, understanding and responsibility. Being able to have a quick divorce is not a solution to marriage or relationship problems. As people work through their problems there will definitely be a stronger family system in India in the future.

The above characteristics and changes with respect to relationships in India illustrate why it is important that great care is taken in choosing your life partner. It is now more acceptable to end marriages, but with that there comes great cost in terms of physical, emotional and financial pain.

While what I have written in this book reflects my life, there are many habits, behaviours and actions that will now apply to Indian relationships. I hope you learn something from this book. I would like you also to experience a great relationship; a relationship filled with fun, romance, happiness, growth and learning.

Choosing Your Partner

2

In India, there is no greater event in a family than a wedding and marks the transition to adulthood. Weddings are a great tradition and involve the efforts of many people.

The personal and financial investment in a marriage makes it important that we choose carefully who we want to spend the rest of our life with. This chapter looks at ways that may help us find that special person.

As mentioned earlier, in old India some engagements commenced at birth. Often the two families had very close relationships and were closely matched. These marriages often led to unhappy lives for both partners in the marriage but many years ago divorce was not so common so the partners usually stayed together.

In modern India marriages can be freer and people have more opportunity to marry who they wish. This allows couples to marry each other if they love each other, rather than if the family or parents approved or influenced their decision in choosing a partner. However, there will be cases where families will often still try to control their child's choice of partner and very often succeed in breaking a loving relationship. It takes a very determined and strong couple to go against a family's wishes.

With these changes there is generally more choice in partner.

> 'Before economic reform, everyone made the same amount of money, and a person's job would not influence my choice of husband. Now Indians move in much bigger circles and are starting to make comparisons, often feeling their spouses are not up to standard. People want to give

> themselves another chance. Everyone believes that they will find someone more suitable, that tomorrow will be better.'

A common saying has been that opposites attract. However, in relationships this is not always the case and research has shown that men and women find partners with many attributes similar to themselves, and that people who are in such relationships tend to be happier. Therefore, perhaps we should be looking not so much at a partner who has the highest qualities but a partner who is similar in outlook to ourselves.

In a country such as India with 25 states, each with its own history, geography, climate, food, language, culture and attitudes, living with a person from a different background can be an extremely difficult experience. Most parents want an easy, happy and socially accepted way for their children. Gods and religion are interpreted differently from state to state so that the whole process of adjusting can be a really traumatic experience.

Research has also shown that there is a difference in what each sex perceives as an ideal partner. Women, for example, often look for a male who has ambition, social status and wealth, whereas men sometimes look for youth, attractiveness and health. Also both men and women who rated themselves highly also had higher expectations of their partner. However, it would seem advisable that we are better off choosing someone to spend the rest of our lives with who has similar qualities, rather than taking the chance that someone who is different will bond with us and make a happy marriage.

Parents in many traditional families, where arranged marriages are still common, often do not understand the needs of their children and often impose their own decisions.

> Rhadi took an instant dislike to the man her father wanted her to marry. The man had a good job, however he had no manners, was unromantic and abusive. Rhadi feared upsetting her father who had a heart condition. "My thoughts were right. The man wanted sex all the time and was quite abusive if I refused", says Rhadi, who returned home within a month of her marriage and

> refused to go back. When asked why she did not protest more before the marriage, Rhadi said "She took a chance with the marriage because I could not risk the shame the cancellation of the marriage would have caused".

In a recent survey undertaken in India, Indian men and women were asked what traits they valued most about each other. Indian men valued personality, morality, health and appearance, whereas Indian women valued morality, intelligence, personality and health. Indian women also were concerned about income, education, occupation and family background. The women placed more importance on intimacy, whereas men's preference was more towards sexuality—physical attractiveness was seen as important.

Both men and women believed that the purpose of romance and marriage is to find a reliable partner with whom that could spend the rest of their lives with. The above therefore shows that there are both similarities and differences in what male and female Indians believe are good characteristics to have in their partners. Knowing the type of partner we want does not make it any easier to find a suitable compatible partner.

The early phase of a relationship is usually marked by excitement and romance, and passionate couples often expect to have that excitement last forever. People will often look elsewhere if that excitement does not continue. As a counsellor in Bangalore states:

> A relationship can evolve and flourish only if you accept others' imperfections. You need to have tolerance. The notion of 100% compatibility is misleading. You can enrich the relationship by giving each other some space for differences.

Women, once marrying for financial security, are now more educated and working in better jobs, freeing them to be more selective. Yet men and women often do not have a concept of an ideal partner in their minds, and are sometimes confused by the notion of an ideal soul mate. Because the early phase of a relationship is marked by excitement, many romantic, passionate couples expect to have that excitement forever. Longing for the charged energy of the early days, people look elsewhere or split up if it does not last.

However, whether we have things in common or not, it is important that both partners have common goals in life. We can also each have our own goals and it is important that these goals are known by our partner so that we both now what we are aiming for. We therefore know what the other wishes to accomplish and what each of us wants. That way we can help our partner to achieve these goals and the relationship then has a common purpose, even if the goals are different. Therefore, we should examine what the differences are and whether these differences will cause a problem in any future relationship. While variety is the spice of life, we need to be considerate of the other person if there are those differences. For example, if there are vast differences to overcome, such as is the case with love marriages between Hindus and Muslims or between Hindus of very different caste status, parents are usually much less agreeable, and serious family disruptions can result.

Therefore, it is very important that we get to know each other so that we know what each wants out of a relationship. Shared interests are very important in a relationship. Without shared interests a marriage soon becomes boring and we soon loose touch with each other and a common purpose within a marriage is lost. Interests do not have to match but it often means that we should explore our own interests together while giving each other their time to explore their own interests.

It is important that each of us understands the other person's expectations within a relationship. We need to try and get a feeling of what our partner's expectations in life are and what the expectations of the marriage will be. Matters such as children, how to raise them, relations with the in-laws, housework etc. These issues need to be raised before a marriage as we may have such different views that the issues need to be sorted out before a marriage takes place otherwise it is left to chance when the marriage starts—this could lead to big problems. In speaking with our partner we need to make sure that we understand what they are saying and are confident that they mean what they are saying. Many people make promises before a marriage and then forget what they had said once they are married. We cannot change a person once they are married, so we need to really know them beforehand.

People are sometimes in a hurry to marry as they are getting older and perhaps have concentrated on their careers. Many couples who are in a hurry don't take the time to check out their partner well enough. We really need to get to know our partner and find out any areas where there may be difficulties and try and sort them out before the marriage. We should never allow ourselves to be talked into a marriage. We must feel good about it and our gut instincts will tell us whether we are making the right decision.

Promises of a rich and prosperous life is not good enough if we are not sure we are doing the right thing. For a start these things may never happen and then we are left with empty promises. These promises are not what a marriage is about—we want to be looking for a lifetime commitment and a loving relationships and not one full of empty promises.

In many cases we want our partner to be the mother or father of our children. If it doesn't feel right then we may have to think again. For many, one of the main reasons for getting married is to have children and therefore if the other person doesn't appear interested or not the type then we may find ourselves raising the children alone. We need to find out what type of relationship our partner has had with their parents—were they close, did they have a dominating mother or a distant father who they did not have much to do with? These things can affect how they relate to people and can give us an indication of how they may be in a marriage.

We could talk to people who know our partner and get a different idea on what they are like. Perhaps ask about his/her background, whether they have been in other relationships, what they are like with money etc. We can then compare what they are saying with what our partner has told us. We are able sometimes to check out their plans for the future with what our friends have heard. It is not snooping on our partner—we have every right to find out about the person we are intending to marry.

We should be able to tell when we have been going out with our partner as to why they want to be with us and possibly spend the rest of their life with us. We should ask the following questions:

- Are they interested in us as a person, or perhaps it is just a physical attraction.
- Is it because we have some money, earn a good living, or be able to get them a good job.
- Are we someone who can help them move up in the company or just look good.

Often we meet our partner through friends, acquaintances or through work. Our social networks are important in finding a partner particularly if they have the same interests and backgrounds. As said before those people who come from similar backgrounds and have similar life goals generally have a better chance of success in the marriage.

Women from a rural background will often find it difficult to meet someone from an urban background. Often they feel uneducated, although they have embraced the urban life. In some cases, their friends from the rural areas have already married, but they feel that marrying someone from their hometown is a backward step. And women from a rural background who have moved to the city may not be interested in marrying someone also from a rural background. This can make it difficult to find an appropriate partner, particularly if both partners have had the same upbringing. Both men and women could become frustrated if the traditional held view that they should marry someone from the same area (rural or urban) still holds strong. However, some attitudes are changing as people move away from the rural lifestyle of having many children and early marriage.

Economic independence both by women and men has helped and this will continue as more people move away from the rural lifestyle. The traditional family unit is changing and is perhaps not as important as it has been when we speak about marriage. As an example, arranged marriages are becoming less common as is the move away from living with parents.

With limited time for dating as people get busier and lead busier lives, how do we set time aside to get to know a prospective marriage partner? In this limited time we do have, having similar socio-economic, religious, racial and ethnic background docs help. However, more important than this though is the level of commitment that each want to give the marriage.

Some working women are also setting very high standards for a partner which makes it more difficult to meet someone who they may be suited to and really love. As well as a good income, an increase in higher education and a greater appreciation for appearances, the standards for marriage partners becomes higher and with the limited time available to find a partner, people may find marriage becomes more difficult. Try and avoid looking for someone who will only give you the material things in life without consideration to the aspects of marriage that are the most important—love, affection, honesty and commitment.

Good relations with our parents often means a better marriage. Good positive bonds that have been established will make it easier in our own marriage. We become better able to handle our own marriage if we have been through a stable and happy relationship with our parents—we know what a good marriage is like and would like to have one ourselves and we are more likely to be interested and committed to wanting a great marriage.

Good communication before marriage is a strong indication of how a marriage will go. If our partner does not communicate well before then there is little chance that they will communicate within a marriage. The strains within a marriage make it harder to get to know each other if one or neither will talk. If our partner tends to argue a lot before marriage then we should not assume that it will change when we become married. The extra pressures within a marriage will only make this type of communication worse and more difficult to cope with.

It is a mistake to think that our partner will change once we are married—we need to go into a marriage with the understanding that 'what we see is what we get'.

Finally, we need to consider the following things when considering a partner. They should:

- have a variety of skills such as good social skills both with ourselves and others—we do not want to become isolated within our marriage and having good social skills is an indication of good communication which is essential in a good marriage.
- be able to display both emotional and physical intimacy and be in good control of their emotions.
- display emotional maturity by being respectful to ourselves and to others.
- have similar interests to us or be willing to participate or be interested in what we are doing.
- have similar beliefs in financial affairs as there can be problems if there is no agreement.
- have effective problem solving skills such as the ability to discuss issues before they get out of control—remember that healthy couples also fight—it is how we resolve our differences that is important.
- accept our imperfections.
- having a strong physical attraction towards our partner is not the only important component of a relationship. Being in love or just wanting to sleep with our partner is not the same as having a loving relationship and we should choose a partner who will keep us safe and secure, someone we have confidence in and be able to communicate easily with, a lover, and someone we can depend on and trust particularly when the times get hard. Of course, affection and intimacy is important and should be maintained throughout the marriage or relationship.

This book will help you have a more fulfilling and long lasting relationship and some of the issues mentioned in this second chapter are expanded upon in this book.

Understand Your Partner and Your Relationship

3

In most cases, we enter a relationship because we are seeking to spend the rest of our lives together and therefore have this common purpose. However, we need to recognise that our partner may have different emotional and physical needs and goals to ours. Our partner may also probably respond differently to changes and difficult times (such as children, having a new job, moving house or city). Men, particularly, place more emphasis on independence whereas women tend to favour greater social interaction—they tend to have more girlfriends that they confide in and have support from. It is also still common for women to place the desires of others ahead of their own desires. This sometimes leads to women having difficulty expressing their own opinions. Often men also believe that it is proper that women should be quiet and well-behaved and this places great restrictions on the way women can act. Also it is not often the natural way for women to behave and this can lead to great unhappiness and relationship breakdown.

In the modern India, there are more and more successful women who are doing well in business and are more successful than they may have been in previous years. It is easier for them to have their own career or to run a successful business. However, because of the older traditions that have marked Indian society up until a few years ago, it is sometimes difficult for the Indian women to show that they are successful as they may find it inappropriate to show up their boyfriend or partner.

These differences as India moves into a more economically advanced country where both males and females have greater opportunities can pose problems within a relationship as each person in the relationship comes to terms with these new roles. In the past few years, there has been a growing tendency in India for companies to lay off male workers over 40 years of age in preference to younger ones. This tendency is starting to rise to epidemic proportions nowadays so that older wives are more often than not the sole breadwinners for the family. This produces an increased burden on an older marriage, so that the wife who likes the material things will start to look a lot harder at the divorce option than previously.

The incidence of domestic violence is increasing in India, particularly men against women. In a study undertaken in 2002, it was reported that 45 per cent of Indian women have been slapped, kicked and beaten by their husbands. The highest rate of violence appeared to be during pregnancy. Domestic violence in India largely was a result of women challenging their husband's right to control their behaviour. It stems from the Indian males perception of what masculinity is about and how that relates to their relationship with women. It appears that Indian men in general have traditionally seen themselves as the superior sex and therefore have control over their wives. Education appears to play a part in that the higher rate of sexual violence was amongst educated men.

Unfortunately, the majority of Indian women who do experience violence remain silent about it through a feeling of shame and family honour. In addition they will often stay in the abusive relationship because they did not want to leave their children and have nowhere to go.

In addition to the above there are cases where women hold onto their traditional values, particularly if a woman believes that they are not equal to their partner and is subservient to them. In some cases this could be by a woman's partner withholding money from them, a woman being unable to choose her own friends or turning down a job because of her partner. Inequality then between the sexes is therefore still a real problem.

These issues can pose a problem in a relationship if they are not recognised, appreciated and accommodated. They can become a real problem in a relationship and we hear 'he/she just doesn't understand me'. We all know of people who know how to push their partners patience to the limit almost to the point that they seem to enjoy obtaining a reaction. It is no surprise then that women become 'emotional' and men complain that they can't understand women. It can be very destructive in the long-term. Unmet demands and assumptions can be carried in relationships to the point that we don't seem to understand our partner and disappointment with the whole relationship arises. This is particularly the case where our demands are perhaps unrealistic—where we look for the perfect partner while also expecting our partner to know what we want even when we are not sure ourselves.

Having an understanding of our partner and what our relationship can bring to both of us will go a long way to providing the intimacy and confidence that is essential while also allowing for that degree of independence that shows we are not dependent on our partner for all our needs. This is particularly the case where the roles between partners start to change for the reasons I have mentioned above.

We need to start by listening to our partner with interest, and without wishing to change them into a person that they are not. Failure to listen provides the message that perhaps our partner is not so important and we don't really need or want to understand them—and listening well to our partner does not take any more time than listening badly. The best way to appreciate our partner's experiences is by listening. This then furthers our ability to understand our partner, as it is then easier to place ourselves in their shoes and view or consider the world from their eyes. It builds confidence as we are indicating respect and interest in them.

We can also build confidence in our partner through our actions such as seeking advice or guidance from them; building confidence in one another should be seen as very important in living together. This leads to our partner feeling secure in the relationship whereas embarrassing our partner will rob them of any confidence, with the relationship dominated by one person. We need to work out what our partner's needs are and recognise areas where they may not be so confident. A recognition and acceptance of this lack of confidence is also an important part of intimacy. We both learn what is important in our partner's life and we learn to respect that.

Our thoughts and how we see different things that happen in our lives can also affect our relationship. If we can change the way we think about things then we have a greater chance of minimising stress and achieving a greater understanding of our partner. An example of this is to be aware that there will be times that we do not have, or understand, the full story behind a particular action or incident that involves our partner. So instead of making a judgement too early or quickly based on what we see or hear which, in some cases leads to violence, it may be worth either asking our partner for more information or the reason behind the particular issue—step back and take a different look at what we think we know. The following is an example to illustrate what I mean:

> A man is sitting on a train after work and is tired, irritable and looking for some peace and quiet. For the past ten minutes there have been two boys playing up and down the carriage not noticing the stares of the passengers. The father is sitting in one of the seats staring out the window, making no move to keep his children quiet or asking them to stop the game. Finally the man has had enough and angrily asks the father, 'Why don't you control your children, they're disturbing the whole carriage.' The father apologises and says, 'I am sorry, but the boys' mother has just died and this is the first time that they've shown any interest in playing—I thought I'd let them go.'

We can imagine how the man who made the comment felt following this conversation. While the angry reaction of the man is understandable he will see the situation differently when he realises that the boys' mother has just died and there is a reason why the boys were playing up. It places a different view on the situation and illustrates that we often do not have the full story. In our own relationship then we don't assume anything with our partner. If we are not sure about why our partner has done something then we need to ask why and do it nicely. There is no quicker way for an incident to get worse than to be critical and angry about our partner's behaviour—we need to ask ourselves before speaking whether it is worth saying what we are about to say and if it is, look at making our comments with a compliment so that our partner does not immediately become defensive or angry.

What so often happens in a relationship is that each party assumes that the other person shares his or her perspective on a situation. We then act accordingly, misunderstandings arise, and before you know it there is a real problem. If we are having a disagreement, we can pause during an argument, and ask for a clarification. We then clarify what we understand our partner to mean and ask if we are correct.

In looking at our relationship we need to consider the way we both see things in life, what we do or do not understand, make decisions and so on. In what is called the Jungian Type Inventory there are four different personality traits that can be used to describe how people think, act and relate to the world. We can read the following, with both ourselves and our partner in mind. It will hopefully provide us with a greater insight and understanding.

These four types are:

Extrovert and Introvert

Extroverts	Introverts
They tend to act first and think later	Think more about ideas and concepts
Require a lot of stimulation	Require less stimulation than extroverts
Like to make or build things—tend to be more practical	Are more aware of how they and other people feel
Are good at listening to what people say	Tend to think more deeply about things—more likely to think through a problem
Like to talk to people	Tend to be less social than extroverts
Favour action and achievement	Not as emotional as extroverts

We can be an introvert or extrovert or a combination of the both. Extroverts tend to have plenty of energy and generally require more stimulation, whereas introverts tend to take the laid back approach—they tend to think before they act. Introverts tend to be quiet and less social than extroverts.

Sensing and Intuition

Sensing	Intuitive
Use the five senses more	See the big picture rather than the detail
Make plans by applying logic and following a clear set of rules	Relies on ideas and inspiration
Preference for data and facts	Tend to focus on the future

Sensing people tend rely on their five senses (seeing, hearing, smelling, touching and feeling) and prefer facts and figures. Intuitive rely more on having a feel for something and tend to focus on the future more so than the present.

Thinking and Feeling

Thinking	Feeling
Interaction with people can be brief and more business-like	More sociable and people-oriented
Tend to research when deciding to undertake a task	Material things are not as important
Have a logical approach to things	Tend to place more emphasis on their feelings when with people
Prefer to use of clear rules or guidelines when undertaking a particular task—ideas are more concrete	Ideas are less clear, more in their head

Those who rely on thinking tend to act or make decisions with their head rather than their instincts, emotions or desire. Thinkers generally have a clear way of doing things and would appear more logical. They tend to like having tasks to do. Feelers tend to consider the feelings of people more and will often be more social. Many decisions are taken using both, but there will be times where one will be more important than the other.

Judging and Perceiving

Judging	Perceiving
Tend to require more structure in their life	Like to look at options—prefer to keep their choices open
Like to make plans in advance	Like to expand their knowledge
Seek to make decisions so they can move on	Make plans on the run—do things at the last moment
Tend to judge people quickly—not as tolerant of people	Tolerant of other people's differences
Tend to be self-disciplined and decisive	Have less discipline

People who are mainly judging look for achievement and results. They prefer to set a timetable in order to achieve that. The perceiving preference tends to be more spontaneous, flexible and creative. They are not so concerned as judgers to have things finished.

Our partner will probably exhibit all of the above traits, however in many cases they will be more influenced by one than the other. If we know our partner well enough we should be able to go through the above and recognise areas where they predominate in or tend to favour. Once again it also depends on the particular circumstances or the issue as there are no rules for each trait.

While the point is not to change our partner's way in which they deal with things, particularly if their traits tend to be different to ours, it is useful to understand the way they may see things. For example, it will often provide an explanation of how they arrived at a decision. If we have a reasonable understanding of their traits it will also provide us with a better idea on how to speak or raise ideas with our partner so they have a better understanding of what we mean or what we are saying.

I have lived with my wife, Wendy, for twenty-one years. I understand her pretty well. I have a good understanding of what she does and does not like, and where her strengths lie. Wendy tends to be more structured than I am and prefers to arrange things in advance, but is flexible and always open to other people's ideas. She is very good at researching before undertaking a task and takes the logical approach, and is one reason she is good at her job. She can be relied on to take the initiative. Wendy is more thorough than I am—she likes certain things in set places, orderly etc. and in this respect I know that near enough is not good enough. She has a good eye for detail, particularly for interior design, colours and so on. However, we can both want things straight away and want to achieve or do something immediately, so there can be that mix of traits occasionally. Wendy is very social and cares deeply for other people, is sensitive to what other people think of her and sometimes needs reassurance—she is a very good and loyal friend and these characteristics help her in relationship with other people. Wendy displays her emotions and relies on her feelings when with other people. She is also a very excitable, energetic person and her enthusiasm rubs off on the rest of the family.

We should also try and understand ourselves so that we have a better understanding of how we approach our partner and interact with other people. We can then see how we match up with our partner, the differences we may have and areas where we may need to improve on.

I am more extrovert than introvert and therefore outgoing and sociable. As a result of high energy levels I can become easily bored with things—I like to tackle new challenges particularly if there is no easy solution. I like to get new ideas and projects organised, but I can rush things. I believe I am very disciplined and is the main reason I have stayed with a fitness and health program for over thirty years. I am very open in my approach to our relationship and will try and be clear in justifying a viewpoint I may have. I enjoy communication and relate well to people—that makes conversation in out relationship very easy.

We should think about our partner. Is our partner more emotional—they may be more understanding if we show how our ideas may affect people or the affect it may have on someone. If we make our ideas more personal then they may understand what we are trying to do and will create a better understanding for our partner. We need to be aware of how we communicate our ideas with our partner, as much as what we are actually saying. When talking to our partner we should look at areas where we can agree with them, particularly if an issue has or is likely to affect them directly. It is important that our partner is aware that we are flexible in our views.

Our partner may not be so emotional however we should still consider feelings or emotions in any issue as they may still play an important part. We may wish to avoid conflict in the hope of keeping everything nice in the relationship. However, we should not keep our opinions or emotions to ourselves for fear of conflict or an unwillingness to express feelings.

If our partner is an introvert and therefore a bit more reserved then we should encourage their thoughts by asking 'What do you think?' This will indicate to our partner that we value their views and wish to include them in our thoughts and discussion. Introverts are not necessarily shy or lacking in confidence, rather they achieve their energy from within themselves as opposed to extroverts who get their energy, motivation and enthusiasm from other people. We don't necessarily assume that our introverted partner lacks interest...they just won't necessarily jump in the air with enthusiasm when we have a good idea. They may just take a little longer before responding or giving an opinion.

If our partner is an extrovert and we aren't we can still show some energy and enthusiasm, communicate openly and bounce ideas around so that they can see that we are also enthusiastic about things. This will help them as they know that we are also interested in what they are doing. Sometimes, the extrovert partner will be more friendly, outgoing and talkative and finds it easy to start conversations. The introvert will be more reserved and may find it difficult to start or initiate conversations—sometimes they just lack confidence. Many of us display a little bit of each of the above—some of us are shy around new people, but very talkative with people we know.

These types of characteristics only start to cause problems in relationships when one partner finds it difficult to open up to the other partner or is lazy in their communication. While this could be put down to shyness, within a relationship this lack of communication leads to a lack of information flow between partners. Misunderstandings and boredom become a real possibility in the relationship as the talking stops.

Some of us will be anxious in new situations while others enjoy the challenge and receive a lot of energy through taking on new tasks. In some cases people do not have a lot of confidence and perhaps their self-respect is low. Having confidence is very important as it allows us to meet challenges, interact with all kinds of people and allows us not to see mistakes made as a reason to stop trying. Confident people almost see making a mistake as a way of learning and gaining more knowledge, and using this knowledge to improve and move on even further in life.

Those with low self-respect find it difficult to let people close to them, perhaps in the fear that any weaknesses that they may have will be open for everyone to see. This will often prevent them from acting or making attempts at things for fear of failing and having other people see these mistakes. These mistakes reinforce this person's low self-respect. A low self-respect in a relationship can result in one partner not allowing the other to be intimate and romantic as they are not confident in themselves.

I have mentioned self-confidence and self-respect as they are very important aspects of a relationship. These aspects are covered in other parts of the book to emphasise their importance and I discuss various ways of improving self-confidence and self-respect.

So we need to look at our partner and try and understand the type of person they are in terms of what I have mentioned just above. The above personality traits have their good qualities as well as limitations. These traits are often difficult to change and I am not saying that we should try to change—for example, if you are naturally quiet then to try and develop a more outgoing personality may be a big task. I know of a couple where the man is more like an extrovert and his wife an introvert, so they have different personalities. Their relationship sometimes face problems as the husband is a type of person who can talk confidently to most people (he is particularly confident in talking to women) and has generally been the more outgoing partner in the relationship. His wife is undertaking some courses to broaden her interests, however she now appears to be uncomfortable with her husband's outgoing nature. In response he is attempting to change his behaviour and trying to be more like his wife and this is causing him some real problems in the relationship and within himself as it is not the real him. This misunderstanding has not been helped by them not sitting down and talking it through with each other. Both partners knew each other well enough before they got married, and they would have known what they found attractive about each other. His wife would have liked his outgoing nature and ability to form easy relationships with other people. It may have even helped them getting together in the first place.

There is then possibility of conflict, misunderstanding and anger, particularly if there is a big difference between each couple's personalities. Some may have a partner who would prefer to sit in front of the television every night or falls asleep as soon as they get home and not communicate, or would rather stay out with friends or work people every night. People with different personalities may attract, however how these differences are dealt with, often on a day-to-day basis, is often important to a successful or unsuccessful relationship. Life would be easier if we all had the same views on life, interests, and attitudes, but there will always be some differences between partners in this area. I mentioned this in the second chapter relating to Choosing Your Partner.

The examples in the previous paragraphs are simply a means for us to recognise and understand some differences while helping us within our own personality. It is not meant to allow us to judge our partner and try and change them—none of us have the right to do that.

It is important that we do understand our partner if they are different to us and focus on the strengths of them—we recognise their great quality, appreciate and learn from them. They can provide a better balance when discussing and deciding on particular issues and they bring an understanding to our relationship, while accepting our differences. They allow a better understanding if there are problems in the relationship. It can also make just living together a whole lot easier.

It is also important for us to examine these personality traits as they apply to ourselves as well, so that our understanding of these within our relationship is easier as we come to appreciate both our traits and those of our partner. I have mentioned some similarities and some differences between Wendy and I. We both work together on smoothing any differences, both consciously and unconsciously—the fact that Wendy prefers things done a certain way is fine by me. I tend to focus on the big picture rather than the detail. I therefore tend to look to the future more and need to be reminded sometimes that the present is also important, but we will both share what we would like in the future. While I consider that we both show our emotions, Wendy is more emotional than I am—she is more open with her feelings, which I consider good as I know exactly what she feels and where she stands on issues and I can respond in the best way.

I have also included a discussion on emotional maturity in Chapter 4. While the discussion in that chapter is principally for us to examine ourselves, we can also look at it in terms of our partner and whether, and to what extent, they understand, use and manage their emotions. This exercise can also help us to better understand our partner.

Understanding Our Relationship

In having a greater understanding of our partner it is also important to understand what we would like out of our relationship—an understanding of the type of relationship we have may help.

In terms of the types of relationships that partner's experience, we just need to look at our friends, work place colleagues and relatives to see the many different types or relationships there are. While we do not live other people's relationships we often help, advise and become involved in small ways as our lives with other people are often closely intertwined. We can see problems happening and we often say that it will not happen to us.

If we do stand back and look at other people's relationships and know what is going on in them, it should be easy for us to also pay attention to our own relationship. While it is not a good idea to compare with other relationships, the way other people behave can provide us with a better understanding of our own relationship. In looking at our own relationship, we can ask ourselves whether it has the following characteristics:

- the freedom to undertake what we would like in the relationship, while giving due consideration to our partner.
- do we seek agreement and understanding, while being able to resolve any disagreements in a friendly and open manner. Do we make the time to deal with conflict and other issues requiring discussion and resolving.
- do we take each other and the relationship for granted and become less interested in each other's lives as it may disrupt our own lives.
- are we able to communicate clearly and in such a way that it does not place our partner on edge. Communication and support are important so that problems are not avoided.
- do we have a high level of physical and emotional intimacy and compatibility, with strong trust, values and respect.
- has our sex become routine with less frequency and quality.
- do we spend a lot of our time dealing with change, crisis and anger within our relationship.

The above are some characteristics we should be looking at in our own relationship. How a relationship works can be changed if things are not working well.

Using the above, I think a great relationship will have:

> A high level of emotional intimacy and compatibility, with strong trust, respect and a close friendship. Communication, support and strong values are important, as is dealing with conflict and disagreement—problems are not avoided and are talked through. The couple seeks agreement and understanding and both help each other out so that one partner is not burdened with all the work. Affection, physical intimacy and sex are an important part of the relationship. Both partners are able to grow, learn and take care of themselves and their partner so the relationship never becomes dull or boring.

This book will help you in achieving the above type of relationship if you want it. Read the above again slowly and try and understand what it means in your relationship and what it may require from you to achieve these things. It involves trust, communication, physical and emotional intimacy and a willingness to help each other out. We can also look at our friends and we may be able to assess what type of relationship they have. This may help us to more fully understand out own relationship.

Understanding both the individual differences we both bring into our relationship and how these differences fit into the relationship as a whole is important. A successful, happy relationship takes time, effort and energy, but it is important that we look at our relationship and see how it is going. The cost in terms of a failure to place enough importance on doing the things that count are equally as large. We will grow and mature as our relationship enters new phases. There will be ups and downs through the life of our relationship, which may include the initial romance and strong physical feelings, confusion if feelings change, resolution of any conflicts and a commitment to each other as these changes take place.

Healthy and stable relationships require trust, respect, emotional and physical closeness as well as recognizing that there will be differences and a need for a certain amount of independence. Most relationships will face the above and we need to determine the extent to which we let the good or not so good dominate our relationship. Standing back and assessing will help us to understand where we are in our relationship.

The rest of this book is directed at assisting you find some of those habits that will help you on an individual and relationship level. Understanding your partner and your relationship will help you with these other behaviours and give you a better feel for why it is important to continue to pay attention to your relationship and to look at ways to improve on it.

Living together should teach us both a great deal about each other, and we are unlikely to find someone else who understands or knows us better. However if, after trying, there is difficulty in understanding our partner on occasion, we accept and appreciate that everyone is different and make allowances for these differences—we should not be angry with our partner for it. A little understanding and patience on our part may go a long way to a similar response from our partner. We cannot and should not do everything for our partner and we should not expect to get everything in return. We need to love our partner as they are.

4

Become Emotionally/ Intimately Involved in Your Relationship

Men and women are generally different when it comes to expressions of emotion, affection and levels of intimacy, with women generally being more open with their feelings. Women will often experience more of all emotions than men. Often the differences between men and women relates to the different skills involved in both sending and receiving emotions. Women tend to use communication and facial expressions to give their emotions away, whereas men tend to hide or conceal theirs. However, men are often not so good in expressing intimate feelings and this often leads to problems in a relationship. Having good, intimate sex then can be a big problem as it is often then seen as merely a physical act or perhaps a duty to perform as couples are not good at or familiar with showing intimate emotions. Men will often be more aggressive when placed in a situation that involves a high emotional involvement or commitment.

A recent survey in India focussed on the reasons for divorce. From both males and females one of the major reasons was the lack of emotional exchange and communication between partners. Often it is the husband's inability to understand his wife's emotional needs and desire for equality that leads to this general breakdown. A survey conducted in Sonepat seemed to indicate that many men are unaware of any household tensions that exist and may in fact be ignoring them altogether while women in this study exhibited a higher level of stress than the men. Ignorance of, or an unwillingness to face, any tensions or problems in a household only makes the problem worse as, in this case, the female feels she is doing it alone.

As Indian people start to think beyond the social customs and traditions of arranged marriages they realize that they have the right to choose their own partner without the sort of social pressure that has existed in the past. Perhaps this gives people a greater chance of finding someone they really love rather than having a partner chosen for them. This can give the marriage a greater chance of being a happy one as each person understands and respects the other person's feelings, loves and concerns as they have that choice to be with them.

Marriage in India then is in transition stage where there is still the old traditions sitting alongside the Western influences. This 'modernising' of marriage has had an influence on the way women perceive intimacy within a relationship. Now, in a relationship, women appreciate and are looking for signs of affection and emotional commitment from their partner and also a willingness of their partner to be able to talk when things are bothering or affecting them. So now the question 'do you intend to marry?' can almost be changed to the question 'do you desire to form an intimate relationship with someone?' Let us hope that is the question.

It is very difficult for women to understand and help their partner who will not communicate and keeps problems to themselves. A woman in a long-term relationship will often feel she is banging her head against a brick wall if she is talking to a silent partner. As well as affecting the openness of a relationship, this type of behaviour can also affect a person's physical and psychological health. It is not uncommon for Indian women, even when their marriages are good, to depend much more on their children for emotional sustenance than they do on their husbands.

Unfortunately, many relationships lack the emotional companionship that is vital, with material and monetary concerns often consuming their life.

The original 'honeymoon' period of early marriage or a relationship may wear off and it is generally accepted that most relationships change over time, however a relationship that lacks emotion, affection and intimacy is a sad one. Often men show their affection by seeking sex—their affection becomes very much a physical act that begins and ends in the bedroom. As mentioned earlier sexual violence in India is also a real problem. Often the men do not get in touch with their emotions and feelings, and the sex that follows is often just about intercourse and their understanding of their partner's needs and desires is lost. Foreplay and intimacy after sex is often considered a waste of time, particularly when a partner is not familiar with it and does not understand its importance.

A survey of college students in India indicated that 54% of males and 42% of females stated that they did not have adequate knowledge of sexual matters and most of their information comes from friends, books or movies. While this lack of knowledge will change as these students get older there still appears a level of ignorance that may not be addressed as people get married.

Many men believe that it is a wife's duty to have intercourse with them and in some cases violence becomes the means for getting this. Sex then becomes a chore for women and a means for fulfilling a physical need only for men—the whole point of the experience is missed and it does not become fun any more. Like elsewhere, as Indian society changes and people have increasing expectations for a more fulfilling life, partners are also looking for a more fulfilling and intimate relationship. Their expectations for this have increased, however in many cases there is not the experience or knowledge to go with this expectation. We all deserve and would like to have a close and intimate relationship with our partner. If you have been with your partner for a little while I would like you to try this exercise below. It concerns what you saw in your partner when you first met them and what made you consider staying together for the rest of your lives. I will start with my wife and I.

Your Early Days

Wendy and I often talk about how we met, what our initial attractions were and what we used to do in our courting days. We met through a close friend—I still remember and can picture the day I first laid eyes on her. Our first dinner out was interesting as the planned dinner cruise was cancelled and then Wendy spilt her coffee all over the table in a hurriedly found restaurant. We both took things slowly as our attraction for each other increased—we were 'in like' rather than in love. We soon began seeing each other regularly, either at lunchtimes as we worked close by or a particular evening. I still remember seeing Wendy at lunchtime and then going back to the office and having difficulty focusing on work—there was a very strong physical attraction. We went away together, driving across Australia and holidayed in Hawaii amongst other places. These and other moments (and the photos to go with them), which may appear relatively insignificant or routine, are the ones we go back to as we re-live our early years. It can be fun, enlightening and a great trip in refreshing our memories. I also believe that it is important for our relationship as we formed an understanding of each other and it became an important part of the rest of our lives together.

You will remember when you first met your partner. Some of you will remember a strong physical attraction that may have guided you towards your partner—perhaps a high level of passion, arousal and excitement. Perhaps you couldn't get that person out of your thoughts and you longed to see them all the time. The times you did see them would have flown and you wonder where the time had gone. Perhaps in the very early days when you were going out these feelings may not have been felt by your partner and you experience the high of seeing this person and then the lows of when you wonder if they felt the same way—you were unsure of their real feelings. It may have been difficult for you to concentrate on things and your mind used to wander. Your commitment and emotional intimacy in the early days may have been low as you tried not to give too much away to someone you didn't really know. Sometimes, a fear of rejection or an uncertainty in relation to your compatibility may have kept you uncertain—you were afraid to be open with your partner.

In many cases this type of relationship moves on towards increased emotional intimacy as both partners become more comfortable with their feelings and are confident that the other person feels the same. Commitment both short-term (boy/girl friend) and then longer term becomes more likely.

You may have been interested in your partner both physically and emotionally from the beginning. You felt close to them and good communication was instant. You accept that person for what they are. The passion that developed may not have been great, as you might have been in the previous example. However, the passion was an important part of the relationship, particularly as the relationship was still young and the excitement of something new was very strong. If this relationship survived over time then commitment grows more likely.

Your relationship may have started as a friendship where you were able to talk about most things (particularly intimate issues) without feeling that there was any commitment between the both of you. You cared about this person and enjoyed their company, felt safe around them and called them when something was bothering you or just for a quick talk. In this case, the level of passion may be low and commitment to a long-term relationship was not considered. Due to your openness and willingness to talk, your emotional intimacy was quite high. This type of relationship can move on to a more intimate level if you both feel some physical feeling towards each other. You started to feel more than just friends.

We can look back on those early days and re-discover what our initial attractions were with our partner—and in doing this look at the highlights and the good times rather than where there may have been problems. Going back allows us to look at where we are in our relationship today. We know what it was like to have a passion for someone, a person we could speak to about anything without fear of embarrassment, a person we could trust and be honest with, and someone who we wanted to spend the rest of our lives with. We entered a long-term, committed relationship because we knew that person and liked what we knew. As we think about where our relationship is at this present moment, but perhaps do not know how to see whether our relationship is good or bad, the above examples may give us a starting point. We all know that relationships change over time as we move through the various phases of life.

I have mentioned a number of those changes in this book including children, family, careers, and financial considerations. So while we may look back on our younger days where the passions were strong and life may have been easier, we should be assured that the important components of our relationship can be preserved or re-captured.

If you still find it difficult to see where you are at, at this moment, and perhaps where you would like to be in your relationship consider the following, called Sternberg's Triangular Theory of Love.[1]

This theory looks like the following:

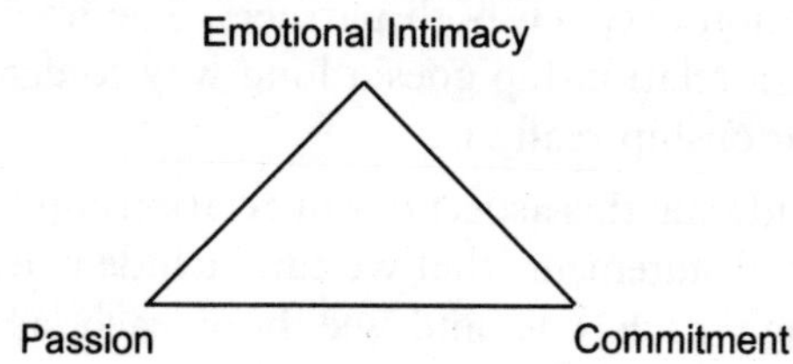

and can be explained as:

Emotional Intimacy: Willingness to talk, being open and honest with our feelings, trusting, forgiving, respect for each other.

Passion: High-level physical attraction, intense feelings, almost excess energy.

Commitment: Devotion, protection, loyalty, security, willingness to commit to the relationship.

Looking at our relationship in terms of the above three aspects will provide a good guide as to how our relationship is—use it as a guide for achieving a great relationship. A relationship in which both partners want to spend the rest of their lives together will have a strong commitment. We will both behave in a manner that reflects this commitment—a desire to see the relationship through the hard times, an ability to adjust to changing circumstances in the relationship that occurs in any long-term commitment, and doing things that improves and excites the relationship.

---

[1] Adopted from *The Triangle of Love* by Robert J. Sternberg.

In many cases people enter a relationship because they are physically attracted to their partner. Passion develops and in the early days it may be seen more as lust rather than love, however as the love develops in the relationship the passion remains strong. It is important that this passion (and there will be varying levels of feelings of it) remain in a relationship for it to be one that satisfies both partners.

The emotional intimacy aspect of the above triangle refers to each partner sharing their innermost thoughts, and a relationship that has compassion and large amounts of support. It is different to sexual intimacy and relies a great deal on the communication between both partners. The level of emotional intimacy in a relationship goes a long way to determining how close a relationship really is.

In considering this aspect of our relationship I have included a check-list of statements that we can include in our assessment. Run through each one and see how each applies to your relationship:

Intimacy

I have a warm relationship with you
I feel that I can understand you
I feel that I can trust you
I receive emotional support from you
I can count on you in times of need
I can talk to you about anything

Passion

I am excited when I see you
My relationship with you is romantic
I think about you frequently during the day
I like physical contact with you
My relationship with you is passionate
I fantasize about you
When I read romantic books I think about you

Commitment

I want to spend the rest of my life with you
I see our commitment as strong

I care for you and feel responsible for you
I remain committed through thick and thin
I won't let anything get in the way of our commitment
I believe our relationship is stable
I don't think about spending my life with anyone else

High passion, emotional intimacy and commitment are what we should be aiming for in a relationship. The passion is there (amongst other things it keeps you both feeling excited in the relationship), we have a great understanding with our partner and we both have the commitment. We respect each other and feel secure in the relationship.

While affection and emotional involvement in a relationship are important and on-going, Wendy and I also find that sex is an opportunity when we can be at our most intimate. Physically that is an obvious statement, however emotionally and intimately it is a time where we talk about our feelings that are generally not expressed in our day-to-day lives. It's a great chance to be at the most intimate level and sex is a natural place for it to happen. So when I hear that people are not that interested in sex (leaving aside any physical or psychological problems) then I wonder if they are missing out on an important aspect of a relationship.

Placing sex as a means for enjoying this intimacy rather than seeing it as a physical act or a chore also means that there is not the pressure to perform physically as this is not necessarily the most important aspect of the experience. There is not the urgency to see who can have an orgasm first and this can help us to relax, enjoy the experience and get better at it. This intimacy does not mean it is all-serious and the fun is taken out. There will be times where you and your partner are very physically turned on and sex becomes the means to satisfy this quickly. However, if you can learn to express your feelings in the more intimate moments then it will take your relationship to a higher level. You will both develop a greater appreciation for each other and a confidence within yourself.

Unfortunately, sex and the general lack of affection or intimacy in a partnership can become an issue serious enough to affect a relationship. Such a relationship makes the partner, who is not seen by their partner with affection or intimacy, feel that they are not very attractive and they probably question their desirability in the eyes of their partner—unfortunately this question is often not answered, and a relationship like that may in fact be dying.

With the busy lifestyle that many working couples face these days, the opportunity or desire to be affectionate and intimate may be limited to the morning and evening kiss. The physical and emotional side of a relationship requires an effort from both sides of a partnership, so that intimacy comes naturally. There are probably good reasons why people have little or no desire for intimacy and these reasons are often related to day-to-day living causing stress, tiredness and perhaps, in some cases, a lack of intimacy and emotional input into the relationship by the other partner.

The 'work hard and play hard' attitude that often encompasses people's lives as they look for both professional and social advancement, can take its toll.

> A wealthy Indian couple in their early thirties, who have been married for five years, both worked long hours, holidayed overseas and had one child. However, they had no time for intimacy as their lives were literally crowded out with other activities or responsibilities. Their sex life was virtually non-existent and they could only manage to devote their attention to one child. Their family commitments weren't the centre of their lives as they spent most of their time with work colleagues or other high achieving friends.

The above example is not that uncommon in a competitive world where the focus is on achievements and material gains. The balance between family and the rest of their lives is lost. You can imagine if, in the above example, the business suddenly went bad and all the couple had left were themselves. The time that they may had for each other has been lost and can then be difficult to pick up after five years of marriage.

A doctor who runs a stress clinic in Delhi has seen a great increase in the number of couples who live in a sexless marriage, particularly where the communication between the couple has broken down. The emotional and physical distance grows between the two and people will often turn to alternative means for occupying their time...or having an affair:

> A traditional homemaker found herself in an affair as she felt like she had to do something about her dissatisfaction in her marriage. 'My teenage children and my workaholic husband paid little attention to me and did not try and understand me. I was surprised that I did not feel guilty about it at all.'

One reason this homemaker did not feel so guilty was that adultery in the usually conservative Indian society is becoming more commonplace and therefore the old traditions are being tested. It is often the case that men who have relationships do it out of lust and a strong physical need whereas women do it to get back at their husbands or because they are not receiving attention. Two very different reasons but it indicates the different needs or wants between men and women.

Any sexual problems could be from a lack of time, lack of energy, lack of confidence, or self-consciousness (a feeling of not being attractive enough). Counselling and education may provide a solution to many problems. Medicinal means will not fix problems in the bedroom of couples who do not get along in the first place and who have no desire or wish to please each other.

Longer work hours, more stressful lives and greater types of communication have made it easier to develop intimate networks outside people's own relationship—and this is often in the workplace. This can often be through flirting on the e-mail system or secret exchanges by text message. It can make people feel good but it will distract them from their relationship.

> An Indian advertising executive, who has remained faithful through his marriage, has romantic fantasies about other woman. He goes to fitness classes and there is usually someone in the class that he likes. As he says, 'I'm happy

> in my marriage but if I don't have somebody I feel attracted to someone besides my wife, then I feel there's something wrong with my life. It makes my life boring.'

As people work longer hours and a greater percentage of both partners working, relationships are often formed more readily through the workplace than social life and intimate relationships at work have a greater chance of occurring. A marriage counsellor in Mumbai recognises this problem:

> 'The office can be a sexy place, particularly as both men and women are dressing and grooming themselves in a more Western way. They are keeping up with trends and are always trying to look their best and it is easier now for people to become interested in other people. However, some people think that emotional flirting with someone at work can improve a relationship at home—it can reduce tension at home.'

The counsellor disagrees with this and sees it as a result of this new era in India where new values, less tradition, and new living arrangements make it easier for people to look elsewhere for a relationship.

It is an easy and convenient way to bring some additional intimacy into our lives without the need to commit to another relationship. It can be problem-free as either person can stop the relationship without feeling guilty as both have probably let the other person know that they have a commitment to their marriage or partner—so there may be no commitment attached to the second relationship. We can all see how it can provide that spark as it's new, there are probably strong physical attraction, and both people may find it easier to be emotionally intimate with another person rather than to their own partner. A lot of things that are new or different are exciting, but we cannot keep looking for this in other relationships—we would never be happy or satisfied.

When we are sharing emotional intimacy with other people that should be shared with our partner and that other person appears to be filling an area that is missing from our own relationship then it is time to question our loyalty and whether what we are involved in is a breach of trust. Would our partner like what we are doing—would they find it acceptable? Added to that is the additional problem that this 'commitment' would have on our main relationship. We think of the time and effort in maintaining a second relationship—if it is because our emotional needs are being met with this other person instead of with our partner then our thoughts will always be with that second person. This will not help our relationship at all and will lead to problems—our partner will certainly notice the difference in us.

You may find yourself attracted to other people and you feel a desire to be romantically involved with them—perhaps it is someone in your workplace. As you also have a loving relationship with your partner this situation can cause some real conflict, as you desire both people. When you are in this situation, know that it is normal to feel attracted to other people apart from the person in your relationship, appreciate that there may be some attraction between you and the other person (if it is both ways) and then immediately think about your partner, what you find attractive about them and enjoy the feeling that you can be in their company and share those intimate moments anytime—there is not that longing that cannot be fulfilled through the third person. You are not then trying to ignore any feelings for other people; rather you are learning to put them towards your partner, which encourages you to think about your own relationship and the importance of it.

Developing Intimacy

Most people in a relationship desire to have emotional intimacy. It's great to have the physical closeness however we all like to feel close in an intimate way. Often this is difficult for people and will take longer to develop. Intimacy is built on trust and deeper sharing. It involves sharing thoughts, feelings, hopes and desires with each other and can be difficult for people to express. It takes time for it to work in a relationship, but both partners need to practice it.

Many books and films these days focus on people having an affair and the romance that this affair gives people. Many people reading these books and seeing these films wonder if the romance in that they see was possible in a real life marriage—they perhaps fantasise that they also could find such passion and they will live in a relationship happily ever after. People now have higher expectations in the marriage and the attitude that sex is only for having children is changing—now it is for pleasure. While these romance movies and novels are very popular in India and provide us with a picture of romantic love, sometimes it does appear easy when other people are doing it. We need to be aware that in real life it does take effort and both partners need to participate. Romantic love is wonderful and those that have experienced it know that it can be the best feeling in the world. Romance and passion are about taking the time to enjoy the company of the person you love. However, for it to work we need to start with the basics and we need to do it today.

Emotional intimacy involves primarily expressing our feelings—they do not always have to positive and can involve our aspirations, fears and emotions. It basically means being honest with ourselves, and our partner. Intimacy does not always have to mean physical contact. The word intimacy is often linked to sex and many people may believe that this is the main time that intimacy is shared. A lack of intimacy in both a physical and emotional sense can lead to our partner feeling lonely and unloved. Being emotionally close to our partner will also help in times of disagreements or conflict as having that trust, security and the knowledge that our partner thinks you are worthwhile will help most problems.

Some suggestions in helping us further develop our intimacy include:

- While it is assumed that we appreciate our partner, we can look at other ways that we may not have considered before that makes our partner attractive to us (and not just physically)—this could be the way people take him/her into their confidence, perhaps a feeling of trust that our partner gives off, or how our partner sets goals and carries through until they are achieved. These in themselves can also make our partner attractive—Wendy was told by her manager the other day that she is one of the most valuable workers in the office and that her presentation, in terms of her appearance, is always immaculate. As her partner this makes me feel very proud of her. I can then think how fortunate I am having a partner like this and the fact that she has chosen to be with me. With this attitude you feel a greater closeness and it can certainly assists with intimacy.

- We can find little things that are sensuous in our partner. These could be things that we have generally taken for granted in our partner and have never really noticed how unique they are. For example, I find Wendy's sense of humour and the fact that she is good at her job and is confident in doing what she does quite sensuous. Building up confidence and self-esteem in our partner by communicating these feelings and we will find someone who we find is attractive in more ways than we thought.
- We can learn to tell our partner what we really think and, most importantly, feel. We look at overcoming any fear that we may be laughed at or criticised or perhaps seen as being undesirable. We may fear that expressing our real feelings to our partners may be seen as a sign of weakness. Often finding the right words to express our feelings comes from a difficulty in working out what we want for ourselves, let alone with our partner. It is important that we learn to communicate both our positive and negative emotions, so that they come out into the open....and we focus on the fact that we both care deeply about each other. We encourage each other to communicate this way.
- We can start by showing some affection—giving a few more cuddles and hugs, hold hands when we walk and begin telling each other that we love them. If one of us is not feeling great then a hug from the other will make the world of difference. Compliments about how each looks and dresses can be very inspiring and adds

incentive for each of us to continue to look after ourselves. A compliment in the morning, such as telling our partner how great they look, will change the way they feel all day.

- It is important that we look into our partner's eyes when making love and learn to talk to each other. This talk can be what feels good, where we would like to be touched and, of course what does not feel so good, how much we love them and how attractive they make us feel. Perhaps we had been thinking about them at work that day and were longing to get home to see them. We can tell them how much we wanted to make love to them. Talking like this will increase both our emotional and physical intimacy as we both share the lovemaking more closely. It also helps us feel more turned on as we share our feelings and thoughts and therefore each partner is not trying to guess what the other one likes or does not like. Emotional intimacy indicates a greater respect for our partner and makes them feel they are not just a sex-object, that we are not just making love for the physical feeling only. In the experience of making love, we see and tell our partner that they are the sexiest person in the world. This will help to enhance our experience as we would rather be there with them at that moment than at any other place. I will talk more about this later.
- We sometimes may need to find a quiet place alone to think about what we want, where we are at in our relationship and what improvements we can bring into it. It could be somewhere we are comfortable with—a walk along the beach, sitting in the park, while we are driving in the car or on our bicycle.

> "Indian men are often not concerned about women's needs, how to express intimacy or even to know what a woman needs to be sexually satisfied", says an Indian counsellor. 'It is the Indian male attitude. Indian females are often trained to think that they are not as good as men and should play a submissive

role in the relationship. These ideas need to be changed for Indian people to experience the full level of happiness that relationships can bring.'

One solution for this is for men to value females sex more highly throughout life, with their wife or partner seen as an equal and important person who is vital to a successful and fulfilled relationship. And this does not only apply to just India or males—there are lessons to be learnt about relationships and this book is relevant to all people. We can all help to make our personal futures brighter and more successful.

We can start by taking time to think about our relationship and whether there are things that could be improved or avoided in the future that will further improve our relationship. We can look at our own attitude to our relationship and see if it belongs to the older days or whether we have moved it into the modern era.

We should ask ourselves whether we have a habit of not concentrating when our partner talks to us, are we easily distracted or find it hard to concentrate on what is going on in our relationship? Pretty simple things but it can make a huge difference to a relationship. In being honest with ourselves we get a better understanding of why we do things that may be affecting the relationship—perhaps avoiding responsibility or alternatively always having the last say in a conversation with our partner, working late or going out drinking to avoid going home. We need to look at these issues. Sharing these moments with our partner so that they have an understanding of what we are thinking is important. As we become more comfortable with ourselves, the way we conduct ourselves, and the way we relate to people on a daily basis, we will bring these habits into our relationship.

- In getting to know ourselves better, we can observe in detail things going on around us, becoming more aware of our senses and feelings. For example, we can try and distinguish smells, noises and appreciate the taste of things. Occasionally focusing on our body and how it feels is a good exercise—muscles relaxed or tense, warm or cool, is our body in a balanced position. Yoga is great for doing this and we can see how relaxed the people are who are practising this. Relax our minds so that we become aware of all of our senses and we can learn to control and improve them—we can become more aware of our partner's physical presence. We will then be more likely to experiment and try new experiences such as enjoying the sense of touch with our partner. It will also help to highlight the important things in our lives as our senses become more important to us.

- We need to take time to listen to each other—while the conversation may involve work or the children we can learn to express our feelings rather than just passing on information to our partner. Even in these everyday conversations people expressing an opinion and saying what they feel is a type of intimacy. Listening will also bring a greater understanding of our partner.
- Supporting each other in times of stress is important. A lack of support during the hard times can make one partner feel very lonely, and resentment is a likely reaction. While none of us look forward to the difficult times, it can bring us closer as we meet any challenge together.
- Most people enjoy talking...about themselves. Most of us, at some time, listen to people with the intention of interrupting with our thoughts. We can practice actually listening to what our partner is saying, occasionally repeating what it is they are saying. If we want to be listened to then it is important that we also listen. Perhaps we can have the attitude that we know everything about ourselves, so if we want to learn anything more then we need to listen to the person speaking to us as they will be telling us something we do not know. We should be interested in expanding our own knowledge and one way of achieving this is to listen to what our partner and other people are saying. We are all in the habit of asking other people what

they think—if we're not in the habit of listening then asking the question is a waste of time as we will not listen to the answer.

Sexual Intimacy

A survey in India indicated that both men and women believed that good sex is important and that they are less likely to stay in a loveless marriage in this modern age—this is different to the older days when people stayed married even if they were not happy. In this survey up to nearly 90% of these women said that they expected, or wanted, to enjoy sex and this is seen in their desire to have equal rights. These women do not want to stay silent on their sexual desires. It is therefore important that special attention is paid to enjoying a good sex life as more Indian couples are seen to be enjoying the entire love making act, from the intimacy that happens before intercourse to the time that partners have with each other after each has climaxed.

Sex drives wax and wane day by day and over the decades. Even so, there is nothing like physical intimacy to maintain and improve a marriage. Except in cases of illness or the time immediately preceeding and following childbirth, I believe it is important that sex be a regular event in any marriage.

Most of us are probably familiar with various techniques and positions in lovemaking. However, within a relationship we often have different levels of sexual response and interest, particularly between men and women, and not being able to satisfy these can cause problems or dissatisfaction in our relationship. It can appear unsatisfying if our particular desires are not met, and I refer to both emotional and physical desires.

Some of the more common sexual problems, both in India and elsewhere, have been too little foreplay before intercourse and too little affection after sex. These concerns were mainly from women, whereas men had problems with premature orgasm and maintaining sexual excitement. A survey looked at the time that Indian (and other nationalities) couples spent in foreplay. The results showed that for Indians the average time was 13.98 minutes, below the global average of 15.78. A more detailed breakdown indicates that 18% of Indians averaged between 0 and 3 minutes of foreplay, 47% experienced 4-10 minutes, 26% experienced 11-20 minutes and only 9% averaged 20 minutes and longer. Even twenty minutes is not really a long time to be engaged in what I believe is the most important part of love making.

What I am suggesting in this chapter is slower, more intimate sex which may provide one solution for those people who do desire more foreplay and intimacy as well as helping men to delay and enhance their orgasm. Sex is not all about intercourse and we (both male and female) should expect to give and receive a high level of sexual satisfaction. We all have the ability to consider our partner while also satisfying our desires. We also need to be able to communicate our desires to our partner—unfortunately to many people it is too embarrassing to talk about sex:

> Although we feel uncomfortable in our sex, neither of us dare speak out about it. It is easier for us to remain quiet about sex, although I think we would both like to try different things.

The reasons for unhappiness between couples may be quite simple, if only communication was effective so that any unhappiness could be identified. We cannot read each other's minds so it needs to be spoken about. It may feel embarrassing talking about what we really desire, or what we do or do not like while making love. Reading books or magazines, exploring the internet or ringing up hotlines to ask questions can help us become more educated and may be more comfortable for people. However, any ideas or informations we may have learnt from these sources mean nothing unless we speak to our partner about it.

And it is more appropriate and probably easier to express such feelings when we are both aroused as we are more likely to listen to and be more open to our partner's ideas in this more intimate time. So if there is that embarrassment then we can start by telling our partner how much they excite us, how sensuous they look naked, how touching their bare skin feels wonderful—in a relationship it is important that we can at least let each other know how they make us feel in these moments of private intimacy. We can then progress onto asking what they like and telling them what we may like. Take it slowly, but look at saying or doing something a little different each time you make love.

You will then be surprised after a while how much more you are both enjoying and progressing in your lovemaking—you will then never run out of ideas and boredom will never be an issue. This enjoyment can lead to greater frequency of sex as it becomes an experience to look forward to rather than a chore. We need to have the attitude that we will never know everything about great sex and therefore it is a continuous learning process, and a process that inspires and excites us to be better all the time.

It is very important both partners realise that they can take the initiative in sex:

> 'We were taught that it is only the man who initiates sex', said Renu. 'I didn't say anything for a long time. However, I spoke with my friends who said that they had had an unsatisfactory sex life until they started initiating sex and telling their husband what they liked and didn't like. I feel as though I could still be married if I also had initiated sex.'

A study in India asked women who initiated sex. A total of 70% women stated that men initiated sex. Only about 25% said that it was initiated by both partners. This is similar to the percentages in the West. This can be for a number of reasons including the fact that men often have a higher sex drive than women and that women tend to be more passive in sex.

Sexual relations between spouses can also be based on a woman's subservience to her husband's needs. If a wife is expected to meet her husband's needs and provide for his pleasures, then often her own needs are not being met. In some societies it is often considered unacceptable that a women refuses sex. Sometimes, a wife's refusal can be seen as a sign that she is having an affair, and therefore to avoid these accusations she consents to sex even when unwilling.

It can also become a habit in a marriage or relationship that men initiate sex to the point that it is the expected thing to do—couples do not know any different and it then becomes routine which can then affect any spontaneity and variation in sex. This study also showed that many women engaged in sex just to please their partners, so perhaps this lack of interest also plays a part—naturally a lack of interest on the part of women will mean that they will be less likely to initiate sex.

India and particularly its major cities, are alive and vibrant. Young couples are acutely aware of their sexuality, internet matchmaking sites have both married and unmarried people, affairs are becoming common, and sexually explicit material is becoming more common.

However, when it's time for couples to have families and to continue with an intimate relationship as well, problems arise. Many couples in a survey said that after their first child was born, the desire for sex vanished. The intimacy or lack of it becomes a major problem—we need to try and recover that.

We need to be emotionally in touch when we have physical contact—this type of connection is important both in and out of the bedroom. We do not need to worry so much about technique, positions and how we 'perform' if we move away from the idea that sex is a mainly physical activity. We can easily find what makes both of us happy, content and excited and nothing is better than hands-on experience. We should take the time to explore what really turns us both on, physically and emotionally.

We want to be totally committed physically and mentally when making love including the appreciation of both our needs and those of our partner so that our lovemaking is taken to a higher, more intimate level. It may not necessarily be easy as we want to satisfy our own desires, however we also want to be aware of our partners' needs and how they respond to what we are doing—often our lovemaking involves the difference between our often strong desire for release and orgasm, with the desire to delay the climax in order to take the passions even higher and the wish of seeing our lovemaking last as long as possible. We need to be aware of how our lovemaking affects our partner, their response to it and being open enough to respond to their needs.

Very good athletes tell us that in their preparation and performance in games or events the emotional and physical aspects are equally as important in getting good results. It is not just a case of getting out there and running or playing to be the best. We want to be the best we can be—to have the fulfilling experience that will have us saying 'how are we going to be able to be better than that next time'—it is nice to think that we can always look for improving our lovemaking so that it does not become routine and boring.

The following are some ideas that you may like to think about:

- We can use our five senses when making love—touch, smell, taste, sight, and sound—and we then learn to both give and accept pleasure so that one partner is not always in control. I emphasise pleasure here as it should be the most important thing in lovemaking rather than how we are performing. We can try making love in a very dark room so that we really concentrate on the feel, touch and smell of our partner as we are not relying on sight. It is also more exciting as our partner cannot see us as well and each move, touch and feel is more of a surprise to them—anticipation encourages excitement.
- A romantic setting in the bedroom and a more relaxed and less rushed approach could be a simple starting point to a more intimate lovemaking. Burn a small candle next to the bed so the light is more subdued and romantic—we also look better in a more subdued light.
- People love to be massaged. We can offer to massage our partner (and you don't need to have training in this) trying different strokes, touches and oils. When

receiving the massage concentrate on the particular muscle or area that is being touched and talk about any feelings or sensations. Feel the tension go and the muscle relax. Learn to control any tension by relaxing that part of the body being massaged and concentrate on taking deep, long breaths—we should focus on our breathing while keeping it completely natural.

The amount of pressure on the skin we use is not great, but go a bit deeper if there are some tight muscles, particularly around the shoulders, neck and lower back—we all suffer in these areas occasionally. The muscles will respond to slow but progressively deeper pressure and hold there for a few seconds before moving on.

As we move around the body concentrate on how the muscles feel and the way they respond to our touch. Some muscles will be harder to massage than others. We can use our whole hand, finger-tips, heel of our hand and so on. Using mainly long strokes, we can also vary it with short ones while keeping one or both hands on the body as we move around so we do not loose skin contact. As a guide massage over an area three times and then move to a different spot. Some muscle groups really respond to massage and feel great. Note these areas and return to them occasionally. The feet are fantastic to have massaged and using oil makes it more pleasant for the masseur—not everyone has great looking feet.

As we do all this we talk to each other, seek feedback and share the moment, so that it becomes our ultimate experience with our partner. It could have been a while that we have actually felt and appreciated our partner's shape and feel. This type of experience can be sensual or it can just be a great relaxant at the end of a hard day where one partner's body just needs a good massage without it leading further. If we know our partner well enough the difference with the two should be obvious from the outset—however, if we are unsure then talking with them as we massage will tell us our partner's mood. It's also sometimes safer to assume that our partner wishes to receive a relaxing time, without the need to move it further to lovemaking. This then does not create any expectation (and disappointment/feeling of rejection) on either side, and we are both more comfortable with the experience. It is surprising how much we learn about our partner's physical and emotional moods through this simple exercise.

As a more sensual massage we can try starting with a normal relaxing full body rub down as described above. Finish with light fingertips all over the skin, with an emphasis on the more sensitive areas—up and down the insides of the arms, the inside of the thighs, behind the knees, the side of the body from the arm pits to the hips and across the stomach, from the neck down the spine along the buttocks and the rear of the legs.

Alternate between full fingertips or just fluttering over the skin so there is barely a touch. Avoid the more intimate, areas for now—this type of movement is very sensuous and allows for a slow build up of excitement and indicates a more caring type of lovemaking. Towel lightly to remove the remaining oil. Once the oil is removed we can then go through the same movements I have just described but this time using our tongue. Run it over the more sensitive parts I have described, varying between longer and smaller movements. As we use our tongue we also introduce some kissing on the skin for variation and also to give our tongue a rest. Both partners can do this together or have one partner lie back and enjoy the sensations and then swap. The art of intimate touching and stroking is very special. Learn what is important and meaningful to your partner, which may be longer touching, stroking and kissing than you are used to giving and receiving, as I have just described.

Massage can also be done fully clothed—it is easy to have your partner sit in front of you while you are both watching television and give them a shoulder and neck massage. We all know how good it feels and the time and effort required is not great. Once again seek feedback from your partner so that you are guided as to what feels the best and what creates the most benefit. You also learn as you go so the experience is mutual.

These simple pleasures of our skin lead me to the following thought: our skin is also an important sex 'organ'. We can learn to appreciate this area of our partner—as mentioned a simple massage is one way to re-acquaint ourselves with the pleasure of touch. We can add to this with appreciating the taste and smell of our partners' skin and our intimacy is immediately enhanced. Occasionally we can try the above with our undergarments still on so that there is not the distraction or urge as we explore each other more slowly. We can re-discover the areas that mean most to our partner without going to the main erogenous zones—leave that to later as we begin to experience the delights of a more 'slow seduction'.

We then move slowly back and forth between this slow seduction, the more intense pleasures associated with the main erogenous zones and sexual intercourse itself. For both partners this experience introduces a more intimate moment as we move away from making love as a purely physical experience with intercourse as the ultimate goal—have the attitude that intercourse is only one part of lovemaking and does not necessarily have to be the most important part. It also does not need to be the final act you perform while making love. As I have mentioned here it can happen half way through making love as we then switch back to more foreplay. The word foreplay indicates that there is a lead up to intercourse. But it does not have to mean that intercourse is the ultimate or the finish of lovemaking. This slower lovemaking I am talking about here is based on our moods at the time but we can with some thought, as a couple of brief examples below show, make some small adjustments that can make a big difference.

So, for example, on occasion the passions at the outset may be particularly high which may lead us straight into the more intense pleasures associated with the erogenous areas followed by intercourse without climaxing, then we can move slowly back into a slower seduction as we experience a more emotionally intimate moment before taking the passions (even) higher again through the erogenous zones and intercourse.

It is fantastic to let your partner know how you are feeling at the various times; perhaps we could indicate the need to slow things down a little if we can feel ourselves becoming too aroused. Slowing or withdrawing from intercourse and more attention to intimate kissing, for example, can help to slow the effort a little while keeping the passion strong—it can also be a great tease as we take our partner almost to the point of orgasm and then slow things down for a moment and then increase the passion again. We may wish to increase our arousal for a short period without intercourse through increased erogenous area contact, so that we can maintain that higher level of arousal for longer but we don't need to orgasm.

We can learn to be in tune with our senses and sensations and by doing this we can monitor and check our level of arousal. For example, we can become conscious of our excitement level so that we can stretch it out for our own benefit and our partner's. The things that turn you on with your partner will change from time to time and it becomes fun to find these out and what level of excitement different positions, strokes, touches and so on gives us.

Following on from this we can adjust our levels of excitement or arousal so that we can achieve a high level of arousal without the need to orgasm. We don't want to become too excited too early as we will want to orgasm.

As our arousal builds, we can learn to redirect our energy up, around and throughout our body so that we can achieve a full body sensation and we are able to achieve a higher arousal level. By redirecting our arousal sensations throughout the body we can achieve higher arousal levels, we can learn to last a lot longer and we can accept higher and higher levels of pleasure.

We can move slowly so that we are more relaxed and we can check our arousal levels and we can focus on the pleasures of the moment. Every so often we can pause for a moment to push our energy around our body. We can breath through the rising tide of pleasure, stretching the experience as long as possible.

For the male, if you feel that you orgasm too quickly the muscle between the anus and the testicles can be used to slow down or stop the release. As an exercise try and contract this muscle by pretending to stop yourself from urinating. Try holding it for ten seconds, rest and then repeat, or do as many little contractions for ten seconds. Do this exercise on a regular basis. As this muscle gets stronger you can actually stop yourself from climaxing by contracting this muscle just before you feel the urge to release.

We can look at varying the physical distance between ourselves and our partner while making love, so that we move between the intensity of being very close as our full bodies touch, and then being at say arms length as we stroke each other so that we both gain a better picture of each other and we can see each other a little differently. This slightly different physical distance can also enhance the emotional closeness, as it requires us both to look at each other more openly because of this slight distance.

We can play and experiment with the above, so making love does not become just a routine activity, and we both become more aware of each other's feelings. We should be guided by our partner as we both enjoy a longer, more meaningful and heightened sexual experience. Both partners need to be fully involved in the experience and this can happen just through actions or we can talk to each other as we move back and forth through the various levels of physical and emotional intimacy. I have given an example of the above in a diagram below which indicates the higher and lower levels of arousal as we move through a lovemaking act. This example can be shortened, lengthened, and varied so that we never become bored.

In what I have said above, the most important thing I can pass on is that we consider lovemaking as the opportunity to give pleasure to our partner. If we focus our thoughts and energies on pleasing and stimulating our partner, then three things will happen:

- Our partner will respond in a similar manner and our lovemaking does not become a selfish exercise where only one partner seeks the pleasure. It is then an activity that both partners look forward to and may increase the frequency in which lovemaking is engaged in.

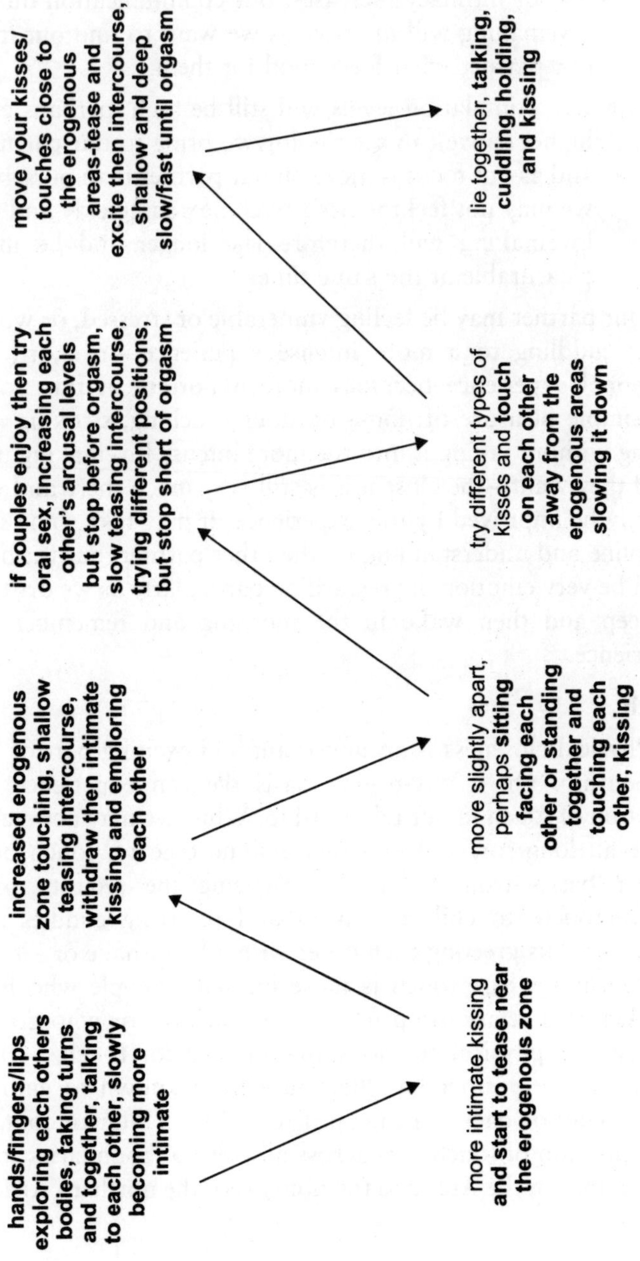
hands/fingers/lips exploring each others bodies, taking turns and together, talking to each other, slowly becoming more intimate
more intimate kissing and start to tease near the erogenous zone
increased erogenous zone touching, shallow teasing intercourse, withdraw then intimate kissing and emploring each other
move slightly apart, perhaps sitting facing each other or standing together and touching each other, kissing
if couples enjoy then try oral sex, increasing each other's arousal levels but stop before orgasm, slow teasing intercourse, trying different positions, but stop short of orgasm
try different types of kisses and touch on each other away from the erogenous areas slowing it down
move your kisses/ touches close to the erogenous areas-tease and excite then intercourse, shallow and deep slow/fast until orgasm
lie together, talking, cuddling, holding, and kissing

- As our intimacy increases, our communication during lovemaking will improve as we want to find out from our partner what feels good for them.
- Our stimulation levels will still be high (perhaps even higher as we can see the joy we bring to our partner), and as our focus is more on our partner than ourselves, we may not feel the need to climax as quickly and our lovemaking will therefore last longer and be more pleasurable at the same time.

Our partner may be feeling vulnerable or stressed, or would prefer cuddling to a more intense experience—in short, the emotional experience becomes more important at this point. The simple pleasure of non-erogenous touching, stroking and kissing without taking it into the more intense lovemaking may be all they want—the closeness is still very much there and will actually be improved by this experience. It may take some self-discipline and understanding by the other partner, but for both it can be very emotionally rewarding particularly as we drift off to sleep and then wake in the morning and remember the experience.

Touch

Physical closeness is an important and exciting part of our relationship. On a day-to-day basis we can experience the sensation of touch in our relationship. While we may not realise it, we all long for, and experience some type of, touch on a regular basis—from babies experiencing the security of a human touch, to children giving and receiving cuddles and hugs, to adults greeting each other with a handshake or kiss, to relationships where touch is more intimate. People who have not been in a relationship for a period of time or who do not have a very physical relationship can long for touch. Older people whose partner has died have been known to enjoy a simple hand or back massage just to feel some human contact. The sensation of touch cuts across all cultural boundaries from the Eskimos in the Arctic to the nomads of the northern African deserts.

Look at loving, nurturing touch in terms of physical intimacy. It needs to be the right kind of touch—knowing how to touch, where to touch in an intimate way without it being a sexual touch. We should be sensitive to what our partner wants in this area as everyday touch is equally as important—an arm around the shoulders for reassurance, holding hands, a pat on the backside, a run of a finger down the nape of the neck, or a kiss on the bare shoulder or neck.

When touching stops between partners then a significant part of the relationship is lost. We can become familiar, or re-acquaint ourselves, with our partner's physical needs and likes and, in the case of touching, respect any personal boundaries and levels of appropriateness while looking at improving the physical closeness in our relationship. The art of touching brings us together—it provides that emotional warmth that reassures each other that we are there for them. A relationship without much physical contact can create resentment and anger and fear that the love in the relationship is dying.

Many people can be afraid or even embarrassed by physical closeness. This is often a result of a lack of affection in their childhood, particularly on the male side where the fathers in the old days were not very affectionate or it was not considered appropriate in public. Sometimes, it was seen as a sign of weakness, particularly where a display of emotion was needed. To show affection in public is also a display that we are proud of our partner and do not mind showing it. We all need to be touched and to feel physically close. It is often a surprise when I see a middle age couple walking down the beach holding hands. It's fantastic but does not appear to happen enough. Often it will leave one partner thinking—I'm not loved anymore, or I'm not attractive. It would be sad if we all ended up like this couple:

> 'My husband never kissed me once and we seldom had sex', said Anita, a cleaner who had divorced her husband because of the way he treated her. 'We had a child, but he never kissed me and we were never romantic. I only learned to do those things after I left him.'

A survey found that more frequent physical affection leads to higher relationship satisfaction and higher sexual satisfaction. In particular it showed that a woman is more likely to be enthusiastic towards her partner's sexual advances if her partner is intimate towards her (intimacy here being hugging and kissing).

People can feel more relaxed about being more intimate with their partner and with practice can become a very natural thing—talking about sex is more common as people are becoming more aware of the joys of sex.

Emotional Maturity

I have looked at various ways to improve how we relate to our partner, including being both intimately and emotionally in touch with them and knowing ourself better. However, all the previous discussion and what you read in this book will be harder to achieve if we do not have an emotional maturity about ourselves.

Emotional maturity can be seen as the ability to use, understand and manage our emotions. As we enter situations and make decisions, emotional maturity is whether we make good decisions or decisions that may just please ourselves without any thought to other people. There are many examples of what emotional maturity is, and signs that indicate whether we are emotionally immature.

The following are some examples that may help to determine our level of emotional maturity.

Our partner has an annoying habit. Do we...

- Try and ignore it as they may raise our habits.
- Explain what the habit is and why it annoys us.
- Worry about what our partner may think if we mention the habit.
- Make some negative comment about it.

Our partner is spending more time than usual at the office. Do we...

- Confront our partner over the long hours.

- Assume that our partner is having an affair and hope that it will finish.
- Talk to our partner about their work and ask if there is anything we can do to help.
- Do nothing as it may cause an argument.

Our partner gets annoyed with us for doing something they did not like. Do you...

- Get upset.
- Apologise and explain our actions.
- Make reference to a mistake they may have made.
- Ignore them as we all make mistakes.

Consider how you might answer the following (from *never* to *always*):

- I am sensitive to other people's emotions.
- I communicate my feelings easily and clearly.
- I appreciate how my actions affect others.
- I am happy to admit to mistakes.
- I can handle constructive criticism.
- I will complete a task even if it is boring or does not interest me.
- I feel uncomfortable giving or receiving affection.
- I find it difficult to forget confrontations.
- I have trouble controlling my anger.

Sometimes, we find that above questions and statements are difficult to answer, or we may not truthfully answer the questions (that is trying to work out what is the best or most 'correct' answer). On the other hand, we may never have asked ourselves how or why we may act or react in certain circumstances or really thought about how much emotional maturity that we may have. Often we don't realise the consequences of our actions and that is something worth thinking about as it can have a big affect on our relationship.

How do We Improve Our Emotional Maturity?

We can go through each of the above statements again and imagine ourself as we answer each one in the positive, particularly those that we may not have scored so well on. For example, we can picture ourselves being affectionate with, or returning some affection from, our partner if this is one area that we could improve in, being sympathetic with them when they are upset (think of some words that will make them happy and which show you understand the situation), or remembering a time where we acted or said something hastily that we now realise may have offended someone but we did not think about it at the time. We should place ourselves in these situations and imagining a positive response or outcome. However, for it to work, the above examples need to be carried into our lives—as I've mentioned in a few places in this book, we all need to listen, understand and slow our actions down a bit so that we have time to look at how our actions will affect our partner.

We see children interacting amongst themselves and with adults. How they act or react in a mature way is limited. I used to be involved in a junior football team and there were always some children who were the first to get upset and blame others if the other team scored. They found it difficult to accept criticism and were usually the first to give up when the team was loosing—often they were the best at the sport. As my direct involvement in the sport reduced I would not see these children playing sport for a number of years and in most cases it was good to see how these children had become more respectable and responsible young adults. They were still competitive but their emotional maturity had made these children into people you did not mind being around.

Our parents and general life experiences usually shape the emotional development of us. Positive, mature parents who love and understand their children and encourage their children to participate without stress or fear of failure are more likely to raise emotionally mature children—we can let them struggle, fail and see disappointment, but we can teach them how to cope with it. As parents we can pass on how to behave well and being an example to our children will also help to make our children into mature adults. Wendy and I are very conscious of the way we behave with each other and we hope our children will learn from our example. We often use ourselves as an example when we speak to our children, particularly in their own behaviour—we may say 'do you ever hear us speaking to each other like that'. Like everyone we have made our mistakes and they have at times been picked up very easily and quickly by our children, particularly if Wendy and I are not consistent with any rules. But we can all try to do our best, which is made easier by slowing our actions down and being aware of the consequences of our behaviour.

We can also look at children for the good and the bad, and use their behaviour as one way to improve ours. Children will always try and get what they want and this is often important to a child's happiness and we will sometimes give in to keep the peace and let them have what they want, whether it be good for them or not. We have all seen the crying child in the shop who wants the lollies and will make as much noise as they can before the parent gives in. They will be happy until they find the next thing they want. Children therefore are more interested in what they do not have rather than being content with what they have.

Adults will sometimes do the same thing as we go looking for the next thing to stimulate us (whether it be alcohol, having an affair or buying a new gadget) as well as associating happiness with objects and things. However, we also know that this is a wasted exercise as we really do not require the constant stimulation or the next best thing. We can help our children and ourselves by recognising this and only seeking what we want if it is really important to us and is necessary. Often we just need to appreciate what we are, what we have and what we have achieved.

Relationships expose us to the full range of emotions. We give and receive love, experience pain, anxiety and suffering, and learn from our experiences. These relationships we enter and sometimes move on from throughout our lives will place us in positions where we learn how to deal with different situations. We can learn to be patient rather than using anger to get our way. Conflict and disagreements are part of personal, business and other relationships—here we need to learn to accept the frustrations that come with our relationship with people, look for solutions and consider other approaches to the problem. We need to control our emotions, rather than letting them control us.

In terms of emotions, inappropriate anger in particular can cause relationship breakdown as well as physical and psychological stress. Many people express their displeasure or frustrations through anger—they can be quick to anger and will often look at physical or verbal violence when confronted with a situation they do not agree with or makes them feel out of control. Sometimes, alcohol is to blame. Children will often hit out or throw a tantrum as a means of expressing their displeasure. While most adults grow out of this, the expression of anger, particularly in relationships, can still be a major problem. I know of relationships where one partner is in constant fear of their partner as they are violent and hope that they do not upset them. Domestic violence in many countries is at an all time high and is often the result of anger mismanagement and an aggressive display of anger.

We all become angry at various times and health professionals believe that expressing anger where appropriate is reasonable and healthy. Anger is often a response to a situation where we may be threatened. Other times it is merely because we feel that our life is out of control. Our expectations may not have been met or people may not have behaved in a manner that we expected. If Wendy and I ever become angry it is often with our children and is from the difference between their behaviour and what we expect from them. However, we focus on the problem or the behaviour rather than the individual—'that was a dangerous thing to do, you could have hurt somebody', rather then 'you're so stupid…'. We can do this with our partner, so that they understand that we are upset with them, yet it is the behaviour or action that is being questioned rather than the person. We never feel as bad or hurt having our actions called into question as opposed to being personally attacked.

We have three choices when it comes to coping with anger. We can express anger, keep it within us or calm it:

- In expressing our anger we can learn to express it in an assertive way rather than being aggressive. Being assertive means making our point in a clear manner so that the other person understands the point we are making and how our needs may be met. It does not mean verballing or physically attacking the other person which only makes matters worse. We need to give our partner a chance to respond to any problem we may have.
- In keeping our anger to ourselves we need to be aware that it can be unhealthy. By not telling the person you are angry with them can cause stress as we keep our emotions to ourselves. These emotions can build-up over time and for some people it becomes too much and they have to let their anger out. Often it will mean that someone else gets hurt through violence or by just being verbally abused. Other people just let it stay inside and this is where physical problems start to happen. In situations like this we need to calm ourselves through slow breathing, see the funny side of the situation or go away somewhere and really let your anger out where it can do no harm to anyone else.
- In our relationship we can calm any anger through exercise or by thinking of something positive. We can make a point to our partner and try some humour if it is appropriate without letting it take away from any point we are making. At times we are all unreasonable, thoughtless and self-centred, so we also need to practise forgiveness if we have been wronged (and this does not means agreeing with the actions of others) as it helps to lift the stress off us as we acknowledge the need to forget and move on—we don't want to hold grudges.
- Sometimes we are prone to anger quickly, so we need to learn to relax. This could mean walking away to a place where we can relax (a walk down the street or in

the park), imagery of peaceful scenes or as a longer term solution become involved in activities such as yoga that teach relaxation. We need to learn to see what sets off our anger and why—if we can feel ourself becoming angry then learning to relax and controlling our actions is the best method.

Good communication can help stop many of the problems associated with anger. Trying to slow down and think about what we are about to say rather than saying immediately how we feel, even when there is real anger there, is not easy but with practice and thought it can be done. We all remember the times when we may have been angry, said something to our partner that may have not been good or not relevant and then regretted it. While an apology will hopefully be accepted by our partner, it may still take time for them to forget the incident. I received the following story the other day:

> Sometime ago a man punished his 5-year-old daughter for wasting a roll of expensive gold wrapping paper. The family did not have a lot of money and he became even more upset when the child pasted the gold paper so as to decorate a box to put under the Christmas tree. The little girl brought the gift box to her father the next morning and said, "This is for you, Daddy." The father was embarrassed by his earlier overreaction, but without thinking he became angry again when he found the box was empty. He said, "Don't you know, young lady, when you give someone a present there's supposed to be something inside the package?" The little girl looked up at him with tears in her eyes and said, "Oh, Daddy, it's not empty. I blew kisses into it until it was full." The father was very upset with himself. He fell on his knees and put his arms around this little girl, and he begged her to forgive him for his unnecessary anger. An accident took the life of the child only a short time later and it is said that the father kept that gold box by his bed for all the years of his life. And whenever he was discouraged or faced difficult problems he would open the box and take

out an imaginary kiss and remember the love of the child who had put it there.

If our partner is angry, we need to listen to and understand what they are saying without becoming angry back at them—we can then respond to their anger with helpful words, rather than saying something that may make the situation worse.

With our own personal relationship we can help improve our emotional maturity by looking at some of the following ideas:

- We can work on understanding ourselves and the way we relate to our partner and people generally. We should not overlook anything that may make us uncomfortable—are we quick to criticise and judge, are we in control of our emotions? Being aware of these feelings is often enough for us to begin to make any changes for the better.
- Understand that a great relationship depends on the emotional health of both partners. While the relationship may appear stable and both partners regard each other highly, some emotional immaturity can lead to one partner not willing to change or improve themselves, which can quickly lead to boredom in the relationship.
- Talking things over with our partner if we have some issues or problems is important, so that we can both look for solutions. We try and take a more relaxed attitude to issues and situations, where anger is replaced by more appropriate ways of dealing with any problems.
- Have a cooperative attitude in our relationship—we learn to give and take and have an attitude where neither partner dominates the relationship or feels the need to impose their ideas and will on the other. Self-centred people disregard other people, while often having a low opinion of themselves. Helping our partner with something will make both of us feel good—if our partner has a problem then helping them

is great way to solve this problem and bring us and our partner closer.

- We can express an interest in what our partner is talking about and give helpful feedback rather than just our own opinion. Asking questions and seeking further information from them on what they are talking about is a great way to keep the conversation moving as well as showing our partner that we are interested in what they are saying.
- We should be aware that there may be times when our relationship has its difficult moments. There will be moments when mistakes are made, when we feel that our partner hasn't been as reliable as they normally are, or perhaps there seems to be a lack of affection in the relationship. As we work through these problems and towards an even better relationship we realise that our relationship is not alone in making mistakes and there will be pain and hurt on occasion. We can face these moments with a new attitude.

In addition to the above, we can also improve our emotional maturity through self-development courses that can improve our social and communication skills, involving ourselves in community activities or groups that develop our inter-personal and creative skills and associating with people who have a positive energy and outlook.

As we become more emotional mature it will be easier for us to express and show appreciation of our partner on a daily basis.

Sometimes, this may all appear strange, however, we can start slowly to allow ourselves to become used to this new way of relating to our partner. It does renew the energy in a relationship and brings us closer. No relationship should be without affection and intimacy.

There are other habits in this book that will also help you develop a more intimate relationship—one that is close and loving.

Take the Initiative—Do the Little Things

5

We all seem to have less time these days as the world moves faster. Labour saving devices have saved time in the household, but everyone seems to be busier. Many households now have both partners working (full and part-time) and, with raising a child or children, the time available to undertake normal household activities becomes limited.

While men appear to be assisting around the home more than they did in the past, surveys indicate that, at home, women are still carrying doing more while also working outside the home. In fact some indicate that half of mothers with at least one child under five have less than 20 minutes a day to themselves.

A study undertaken in Australia by Victoria University looked at roles by men and women surveyed men about their spare time. It found that a lot of their leisure time was spent watching television, playing video games or generally not doing a lot. In summary it found that those surveyed did not spend time engaged in much meaningful activity, were often lonely and may almost 'die of boredom'—there appeared to be some connection between these circumstances (and the emotions and possible behaviours such as drinking) and an increased risk of death. On the other hand, women appeared to busy themselves with domestic chores (including a greater share of child caring) and a greater pursuit of life experiences. The study suggested that, for this reason alone, there may be good reason for men helping to a greater extent in this type of unpaid work. The following perhaps explains some of the situations in Indian households:

> Every household and the situation with every female is very different, and they can't be forced to follow a single pattern. For example, some women particularly enjoy and are skilled at taking care of children, and some men also have this love and talent. On the other hand, some women particularly like to work outside the home, and have little interest in home management. If this kind of woman is forced to stay at home for ten years to assist her husband and educate her children, not only might she not perform household chores well, she might also feel psychologically unbalanced. Women have equal natural gifts and abilities as men in fields outside raising children and doing household chores.
>
> Many people think that women are the best to carry out the duties at home, which may have been the situation before society reached today's stage.

Another study that compared American and Indian husbands showed that husbands in India do very little housework—much less than American fathers—and they are rarely do any handyman work around the house. Indian men's work and family lives were found to be relatively independent. They rated their work time as more important than home life, but they felt less engaged, more content and in control of their time while at home. They also viewed themselves as the leader across all family interactions.

In Japan, where relationships are going through similar changes, there is a men's group called 'Men in the Kitchen', where men are taught how to shop, cook and clean for themselves. One Japanese gentleman now does the dishes and cooks for his wife at least once a week. "I will never forget the look of happiness in her eyes the first time I cooked a meal while she was able to sit and read a book", he said. The man's wife now speaks approvingly of her husband, to the extent that she spends more time with him than going out with her friends as she used to do just to avoid her husband.

Equality of the sexes is becoming more common in Indian society. Two income families is common, and will become more common as India moves ahead economically and there are more opportunities for good careers. The Indian male is showing his feminine side in areas beyond personal grooming. Across society, differences between the genders are blurring specially in the urban markets. It is increasingly accepted and expected that women will display traditionally masculine traits, such as competitiveness and aggression, alongside more feminine values and roles.

However, surveys reveal that women continue to be responsible for family duties such as housework, child raising and caring for the elderly. In some cases if there is conflict between family and career, family comes first. As a female in Mumbai states:

> In a joint-family—rural or urban—a woman, even when she is working, has to perform multifarious household chores. The range of her functions is from being a cook in the kitchen to a principal in a school or a college. Her life is a tale full of stresses and strains of home and office. So much so that during the time of her leisure and pleasure, she has to carry the 'home' wherever she goes.

The exact volume of work at home depends on some of the following factors:

- The size of the family.
- How much each member contributes to household work.
- Whether there is any outside assistance available.
- The quality or standard of work expected in the household.

In the West there is often a well-defined pattern for getting the household chores done. The contribution from each member will vary, however, as more households do have two income earners these patterns have become even more defined.

With India, priorities have shifted in a country that has been very strong on tradition. As mentioned earlier the priority has usually been with the husband, however, for women the change has been towards their careers and there can be problems when the husband is not willing to help out at home when his wife has also a career to think about. For men, often their primary dedication is to their work and the family comes second. With women becoming more involved in education and the new economy, the possibility of conflict arises as there is usually a division of labour at home. This is not helped by women wishing to maximise a career path within their twenties or thirties when having children is also a consideration.

Getting married and then giving birth to a child will change the life of a woman, particularly. It will challenge the kind of independence that they may have valued most—baby's crying and endless housework may mean that an ambitious woman has to surrender her aspirations for a rewarding career to cope with everyday housework. Demands can take up all their time and energy and prevent them from doing what they really wanted to do and from going wherever they wanted to go. It does become a real problem when the following situation occurs—*we both have our work and we both work outside of the home. Why can't we share the household chores so that the load for me can be reduced.*

Women who stay at home and have given up good careers to be mothers and homemakers can find this new role daunting and boring as they tend to the demanding role of being a mother and also have to face the drudgeries of housework. While some argue that women choose to have a baby, it is a joint decision and if the woman has been a career woman, the husband needs to realise that the woman is making some sacrifices by staying at home. Help around the house goes a long way to relieving the stresses that can build up through the day.

While I mentioned earlier that the sharing of tasks at home is becoming more common, unfortunately many husbands, in both India and elsewhere, and particularly those from the older generations, think and believe that to help with household chores somehow diminishes their masculinity and that they lose face in the eyes of family and friends if they share the tasks in this way. These ideas can become entrenched in the male mind-set so that they will even defend their inactions with the excuse that it is "women's work". It is important that we realise that saving face with our peers when it comes to household chores will be detrimental to us if at the same time we lose face with our partner at home and our marriage suffers overall.

There is therefore the real possibility that people in India, particularly women, will become trapped by domestic responsibilities as well as career demands as the country develops further and little assistance is offered at home. A marriage relationship should remain balanced if both partners are to feel happy and fulfilled. Partners should not feel guilty about trying to pursue a professional career because the household chores get delayed and there is not some assistance at home. It is important that both partners are able to pursue self-development without exhausting themselves. To assist this then this chapter looks at various ways that the chores at home can be shared so there is that balance and both partners will be happier. This happiness then helps in the relationship—a caring, helpful partner is also a more attractive partner who can also assist in the physical side of the relationship. Of course if one partner is at home full time then the household chores should be their main responsibility.

We can then consider assisting in areas or ways that we haven't done or considered before. Helping with the household chores for example are the little things that can make a big difference. If there are children then, for the men, being a 'hands on dad' takes the strain off our partner as children can be very time-consuming. The rewards of playing with and spending time with our children is enormous and can never be replaced—the time lost not participating in their upbringing can never be re-gained.

Individually these tasks around the house may not take a great deal of time but added up can seem like a lot of time—and someone has to do the work, so we need to consider sharing the work. And we don't need to offer to do the task as we may get the response 'it's okay I'll do it in a minute' and so we leave it. We just do it and we should not go looking for or expecting praise—we will probably get it anyway from our grateful partner.

In trying to balance work/home life the household chores are the second biggest user of time after paid work. It is almost like a second job and for many it can be a case of getting home and starting all over again with work. Many partnerships will have their own routines worked out, from which days certain areas are cleaned to who does the cooking or cleaning up. As well as the major tasks around the house there are also the day-to-day jobs that require doing—and this does not include looking after ourselves, so it is not a surprise that people appear to run out of time. Time constraints are one of the biggest obstacles to achieving what we want to achieve.

Running the house is a little like running a business. When a business runs smoothly there is a lot more time for the important things such as business planning, expansion and customer relations. These are the things that could mean the difference between business success and failure. If we can get the small things done then there is greater opportunity to keep our mind on running a good business (or good relationship).

In doing the small things at home we all acknowledge that chores are dull and repetitive and can be one reason why they're not shared. Tasks around the house should be a shared responsibility, particularly if both partners work. After money, conflict and arguments over tasks around the house rates as one of the most significant reasons for relationship problems.

In sharing the load around the house, what we want to be looking for is a fair share. Therefore, if in our relationship one of us does not like cooking for example then that person could clean up and perhaps do the laundry. We can try and find where we are both satisfied and one does not feel taken advantage of, and we can look at swapping as chores can be boring and repetitive and even some variation makes a difference. Picking up some cooking skills will help us if our partner is sick or unavailable to do it—we may also discover that we have a talent for cooking. It's also a nice surprise if we decide to prepare something—food always tastes better when prepared by someone else. Wendy enjoys cooking and during the week she finds it helps her forget about work at the end of the day.

However, like anything, there are times when she appreciates a break from it.

Our children also have their tasks to do and they swap every week. They also have an understanding (although they need to be told most days) that they do not play until their rooms are tidy.

A home that looks tidy (and it does not necessarily have to be spotlessly clean) is not difficult to achieve if everyone learns to put away their own things. That is the key—being responsible for our own things. In most cases it is a small contribution each day, but if it becomes a routine or habit it doesn't feel so much like work.

If we do not have a routine of undertaking chores in our household, it can cause stress and misunderstanding and can appear to be inequitable. The general sharing of care, leisure, financial and household chores requires discussion within the family. It can be difficult for this to take place in a society that has traditional roles for men and women in work places, communities and families. Men are traditionally the breadwinner and women have undertaken the caring and nurturing at home. Any changes to this will require some work within the family. We can consider the following ideas:

- We can sit down with our partner and work out a program for the care and running of our home—for example, we can think about setting a standard for how clean and tidy the home should be, what each like or would prefer to do and what each partner is good at (one may be better at for cooking for example).
- Both partners should agree that constant reminders to share the workload is not good and produces tension and sometimes anger in the relationship. Both partners should agree that taking the initiative is far easier than having to be directed or nagged and this should be the best way of cooperating around the house.
- We can work out what we don't like doing and look for the best solution in undertaking these tasks. This may be a task that we both already avoid. Take turns

or do it together if it is possible. Companionship while undertaking tasks will help to make the jobs not so boring.

- We can determine whether it is more suitable to do the major chores of the home on a particular day, say a Saturday morning, when we can both do them together or do them during the week. For example, Monday clean the bathrooms, Tuesday clean the floors and so on. Most days will also involve small cleaning jobs, laundry, and tidying up which can also be shared.
- We should agree on a list of duties that each will undertake. See whether these duties can be swapped and, if so, when, and have some arrangements if one cannot undertake the task. If one of us is the chief cook and for some reason cannot cook the meal at a particular time then be prepared for this situation and perhaps have the other partner do the cooking.
- It is a good idea if we let each other know of events, meetings, etc. in that week that can upset some of the planning. We can then work out a solution early so the issue of, say, cooking, or another task, does not become a problem or something has to be arranged at the last moment. Wendy and I had a routine for picking our daughter up after work. There were times when one of us had something on which meant that the other person would also have to make an adjustment to enable Charlotte to be picked up. Flexibility is the key here and nothing should be so urgent or important that family comes second. However, do have another plan if an emergency does arise.
- If some of the tasks around the house are not getting done then we can sit down with our partner and discuss it together. See if there is a reason why one partner is not helping with the work and find out the reason. Finding out who is to do what work in the house involves a certain amount of trust in each other and so a failure to follow through by one person shows

a lack of respect. The partner carrying the load could carry on, with some tasks either not getting done or being completed at a later time. This can have a long-term effect with one partner eventually taking over the majority of tasks because the other won't. If our house starts to go this way we can consider the following:

- Thinking of ideas that may help our partner become interested such as suggesting that the work be undertaken to his/her favourite music so there may be some inspiration to start and complete the work, or rewards for completing the task. I know Wendy plays some of her favourite music up loud when she cleans or puts on a video when ironing. Have times to complete particular tasks and see who can break the record for the time to do it—make a bit of a game of it.
- Hiring help to undertake some of the jobs, but this can be expensive and not many people can afford this.
- Put a list of each person's tasks on the fridge and mark off yours as you do them. A reminder that our partner can see may be all that is required for an action from our partner.
- Cutting back on some of the jobs that perhaps aren't so necessary—in looking at our standard of housekeeping it may be possible to do with less, or not be so strict with our standards. I worked with a lady who was more than happy for her son to hang out the washing—he could hang it any way he wanted as long it didn't create extra work (by this she meant that it meant more ironing because he did not hang them out properly).
- Becoming even more efficient at doing the tasks—do them quickly but well (see how quickly you can clean the bathroom/s) and try multi-tasking such as doing the little bit of ironing you while dinner is being cooked. Perhaps cook a few meals at a time

so that there are meals ready to be heated up when you need them.

- Make less effort on tasks that we undertake that may affect our partner (for example, ironing)—the inconvenience may be enough for our partner to think that they should help out. Having set the guidelines between the two of us some commitment should be expected. Like many things in life, if a commitment is not met then there are consequences to be felt by the other party. Our partner needs to be made aware of these consequences, however, changes are less likely if we continue to help them by doing all or most of the chores. Be assertive and look at those tasks that will have the most affect on them and say—'look I'm sorry, but as you won't help by tidying up after yourself and I'm having to do it, it is difficult for me to get the ironing done when you need your shirts'.
- Be aware that leaving things to the last moment motivates most of us—things get more important the longer they have been left and eventually even the most boring task will get done. We could try being patient with our partner if something remains undone and see how long it takes before they experience the affect of them not doing the chore. We shouldn't step in too quickly to do the chores for them as they will then never do them.
- If possible we involve our children in the maintenance of the home—we set them tasks that they are capable of undertaking that won't require us to closely supervise. The reward of pocket money always helps, however, apart from helping us, it helps to provide them with some responsibility.
- Look at ways or systems that can create reminders for jobs to be done. Apart from the fridge door, look at a bulletin board or on the calendar where messages can be left.

There will be situations where one of us does work long hours, has a particularly physical job, or the hours worked are not standard (for example, taxi drivers, shift workers) and therefore it is not so easy to split the tasks. Once again a solution that means each partner does an equal share should be reached taking account of the particular circumstances. In all the running around that is needed to keep our home running smoothly, we should try and keep at least one day free of work. For most people this will probably be on the weekend. Spending it as family time, catching up with friends or just taking a break from what we normally do during the week helps us to recover and we will not feel we are working all the time.

We should appreciate that not everything will get done in the time we'd like. We can't be too hard on ourselves, or our partner, and as we learn to concentrate on the important things. We will appreciate the additional partner and family time that results from cooperation and sharing around the home, in addition to having an appreciative and not so tired partner. We will both welcome the outcome and it also indicates a respect for each other. If children are involved it will teach them responsibility and, while they may not realise or appreciate it, gives them a greater involvement in family life. In one way all this helps us both to become more involved in our relationship. The next chapter takes this involvement a little further.

Taking Care and Improving Yourself

6

It is acknowledged that as we age most of us put on weight and our general physical appearance and often our health suffer. So some years into a relationship can bring out some significant physical changes. This applies equally to women as well as men. As people age there is loss of some energy and physical attractiveness and we slow down. However, with an appropriate exercise program and general healthy living there is no reason why the ageing process cannot be slowed down. Apart from financial concerns, people over fifty see the ageing process as a major issue in their life. It's never too late to start—we can have the attitude that we want to get better, not older.

Indian people have always enjoyed a wide range of recreation activities such as swimming, badminton, volleyball, cricket and hockey. Like people in the West, Indian people, particularly in the urban area are living longer with the life expectancy rising. More and more Indians are turning to gyms and health clubs.

However, the physical fitness of those Indians who are becoming richer becomes worse after they turn 40 years of age. Obesity is becoming more common amongst adults as well as younger people. The influence of television, computers, cars, western diets and longer working hours has meant that the average urban Indian is less active than only a few years ago. Also people from urban and high-income areas are now more likely to consume a high fatty/high meat diet, which in the long run can cause serious health problems such as heart disease and diabetes. In the urban setting more people, both males and females, are in jobs that require little physical exertion compared to those in the rural areas where there is more exercise associated with earning a living. The Indian population can generally be divided into three categories—the upper affluent, the middle class and the lower poor class. The health problems likely to be met by the upper affluent include diabetes, obesity, hypertension and cardio-vascular disease. The prevalence of overweight and obese people is highest in the northern states of Delhi and Kerala, where about one in five are overweight or obese. A survey by the All-India Institute of Medical Sciences found that 76% of women in New Delhi were suffering from abdominal obesity.

Taking care of ourselves is one area where we all have the ability to undertake almost immediate improvements, and these improvements are very real, can have a dramatic effect and they do provide the incentive to continue to look for improvements. If then we consider that our lifestyle at this moment is a little routine, we are perhaps not at our best and we would like to somehow improve how we are, then we can look at this habit as a starting point for possible changes. Any improvements in ourselves will help us in our relationship as we become more confident in ourselves.

Making an effort in having a healthy lifestyle and taking pride in our appearance should make us more appealing to our partner and to ourselves. Deep down we all desire to be physically attractive (for most people, when we look at another person it is often of their physical presence/appearance) and is one reason that many people are, or have been, on diets. Whether this attitude is right or wrong, a number of Indians (both male and female) surveyed about body weight indicated that being overweight was the fastest way to get rejected. Some of the women stated that Indian women are expected to look like Bollywood stars with perfect figures—'The size zero, straight hair, freshly plucked, and waxed is idolized.' The Indian woman also generally has a different body shape to her Western counterpart (fuller breasts, not as long legged and more defined hips, for example) and often they strive to achieve a different type of body because that is what the fashion or advertising industry dictates.

How we see our bodies and health and whether we are comfortable with the way we look (and feel) is up to each person and I am not saying that being fat is bad and thin is good. We all have different ideas of what we consider is attractive and healthy looking. We often look towards celebrities and high profile people as a guide to what looks good. We also have different ideas as to what we want to achieve in fitness and health—some people are quite happy how they are now, as long as they can carry out their day-to-day tasks and perhaps be able to play and interact with their children. Being thin as the ideal body type is a relatively new standard in India, a trend occurring because of increased wealth and media exposure to Western lifestyle. Indian youth's unhappiness with their weight is significantly related to what is read in magazines or seen on television, leading people, particularly women, to adopt such unhealthy behaviours as smoking, drinking or unhealthy eating. The message in the media is often that men need to be powerful, athletic, rich and confident, while women are portrayed as beautiful, with shining glossy hair and glowing skin. For most of us, this 'ideal' is difficult, if not impossible, to achieve.

I know many people who are not happy about being seen in a swimsuit, for example. Few people, particularly women, are happy about the way they look in the mirror—many women see their bodies in terms of physical attractiveness and how they look is often how they feel about themselves. Perhaps unfortunately, body attractiveness is highly valued and has an important impact on many individual's physical self-confidence, and this self-confidence can affect our self-esteem. It can therefore have a very powerful affect on us and our relationship. It is important that we avoid unhealthy thoughts about our body and appearance. We should be aware that the so-called ideal shape that we see on television and in magazines is unrealistic because we all vary in body shape, size and genetic make-up—often the 'healthy' images we see are often the result of unhealthy and bad living habits. Many of the female models are on drugs or extreme diets. We therefore need to be careful what we see in magazines and on television.

Having a good appreciation of ourselves and following a healthy lifestyle can improve self-confidence and self-respect, which can only improve our relationship. More importantly, improving our health also increases our energy levels and generally helps us perform better in most physical tasks and assists us in fighting illness and the ageing process. With this increased energy that we have comes a greater feeling of being sensuous and appealing to our partner. Its okay to feel sexy and sexual desire is often stronger when we are in good physical shape—and it certainly makes us feel more comfortable and confident within ourselves. So there are very good reasons for taking care of our bodies.

As a partner in a relationship there is, I believe, a certain responsibility for us to take care of ourselves, for two reasons:

- A partnership requires two people to work properly. If one partner is unhealthy, unhappy or does not look after themselves and has a poor self-image then the relationship can suffer—we should give a relationship every chance to be a happy one.
- For each individual our moods and feelings about ourselves are related to doing the things we enjoy and also how we cope with tasks and jobs that need to be done, particularly those around the house. Being healthy and energetic will assist us to achieve these things, particularly as society becomes faster and people try and achieve more. If we take better care of ourselves, we may also consider ourselves to be more valuable and our self-respect is higher. If we value ourselves our attitude towards our partner should be increased and we will also take better care of them.

Having an understanding of both the physical and mental aspects of looking after ourselves is not easy, but it puts us in a good position to progress both physically and mentally.

Ageing

As people age the following changes often occur, to varying degrees:

- Lean muscle tissue decreases—strength decreases resulting in posture and joint problems, reducing our ability/capacity to undertake tasks.
- Fat deposits increase—cardio-vascular disease, diabetes and other lifestyle conditions increase.
- Body shape changes resulting from the above, with males depositing fat around the abdomen and females depositing around their hips, and positive body image decreases.
- Metabolism decreases—increase in fat build-up.
- Aerobic capacity decreases—less effort is made to exercise or maintain exercise.
- Muscular/skeletal system wears down—mobility becomes affected, arthritis and other joint problems increase.
- Flexibility decreases—stiffness and less mobility in the joints.

The above is not a pretty picture, but we all have to face it—how we deal with ageing and how we manage it is what counts. As we age and our fitness levels reduce so, in general, our energy levels drop. Our skeletal system weakens and joints start to wear yet for most of us our weight increases as we get older—this increase in weight places additional stress on an already weakening skeletal system, so we are making it worse. People then move less and the effort to start and maintain a healthy lifestyle program is greatly reduced. We sometimes see the benefits of starting an exercise or health program only after doing it for a while and this can stop people from continuing their program as they do not see short-term benefits. Many of us have seen the affect of ageing and poor health on our parent's health and lifestyle.

Why don't People Exercise?

The reasons for people not participating in fitness programs or not undertaking their own measures to improve their health are not easy to say. There are many reasons why people have nutritional problems, find it difficult to control their food intake and attempt diets. It is the same for general fitness. Each individual has different ideas of what fitness means, how they see themselves physically and why they will, or will not, undertake some kind of exercise program.

Being inspired is seen as one of the requirements in undertaking and continuing with a fitness and health program. Be inspired to improve by looking at role models in the area; people who have achieved and are getting the benefits of being fit and healthy. Be inspired to follow what they are doing. I recently watched a couple on television who were in their eighties, performing a type of ballet/dance routine while a rock band played next to them. They were clothed only in their underwear. It was particularly inspiring—their strength, flexibility and ability to move with little or no restrictions were fantastic and the crowd watching thought it was amazing. I went for a bike ride that afternoon and I was inspired by those two people I said seen and it will be something that I will remember when I am looking for a little inspiration when I am exercising.

When deciding to get fit and healthy we should be aware that little distraction and things such as illness, holidays and work can interrupt any program and often provides an excuse not to undertake or continue it. We have to be able to keep focused on goals. When exercise programs such as walking on a daily basis do not provide significant and fast changes to someone's well-being and body, then this becomes another factor or reason for people to easily stop their exercise program—'it wasn't really helping me so I decided to stop'.

Here in the West we often look at slimming pills or the latest diet or exercise machine for the home that can offer quick weight loss. We believe it is these simple and quick solutions that will solve our every weight or health problems—many drug companies are trying to come up with pills to help us loose weight. Bad diet, smoking, stress and lack of exercise cannot be fixed by a pill, and often these quick solutions have side-effects that affect our health. Any fitness and health solutions will therefore take time to work and will take discipline. Probably the most common reason people do not participate is the perceived lack of time or they are too tired:

> 'I come home from work and I am tired and all I want to do is sit down, watch some television and eat my dinner', says a Mumbai office worker. 'I don't want to worry about going out again to exercise, if I don't have to. I can still do my job and therefore it doesn't really matter if I am not fit.'

Becoming and staying unfit then becomes a vicious cycle:

> 'My son has become overweight because he eats too much. He then does not do exercise because he says it is uncomfortable, and then he puts on more weight because he is lazy. I just want him to go outside and run all the food off.'

Children are not always the best judges of what is good for them. They sometimes need to realise that a walk to the park with some friends after school for a play and run around is all they need to reduce weight. Exercise is available to everyone—it is just that many people just don't take advantage of it.

We should look at the athletes competing at the Disabled Olympics who, despite some enormous limitations, train and compete at the highest level. I have witnessed men and women in their eighties who have either commenced or are continuing with exercise programs. Their quality and contribution to life is still high, mainly because their attitude is that their real age is not important and the energy they receive from their exercise program allows them to continue to enjoy life at the highest level. So really, there are no excuses.

Achieving a good level of health and fitness will go a long way to improving our self-respect and confidence. With this increase in self-respect we become proud of ourselves and this has a great bearing on relationship with our partner. Imagine we have little self-respect, perhaps we do not take a lot of care with our appearance, or our sense of achievement is low—we start to feel depressed. We might continue to smoke and perhaps drink heavily even if we know it is not good—we know we could be doing better because we can change these habits, and we are the only one responsible for them and the only one able to make the change.

If we thought about it our trust in ourselves would probably be low as we know we can't give the unhealthy things up that we should—perhaps our discipline is low. Many people at this level will use excuses to justify where they are at—'I do this (smoke, drink etc.) because I am stressed and I need the relief' or 'I am at an age where it's normal to put on weight and therefore I can't really help it'. If we are like this it would be no surprise if we are also not confident with our partner. After all, if we cannot be good to ourselves then how we will be supportive and interested in what our partner does or thinks?

Where to Start

With all the pressures on modern day life and the general feeling that people do not appear to have enough time to devote to themselves, it is not surprising that fitness and health is not seen as important. It can be easily overlooked as it takes time, discipline and inspiration to commence and maintain. If we find ourselves in this situation consider the following:

- Admit that we are not fit or healthy, or could become fitter and healthier.
- We view our fitness and health as an investment in our future, and not a chore that has to be done—we enjoy this commitment to our future as we consider what we have the potential to become.
- We can develop action plans to assist ourselves in undertaking an exercise program so that we know exactly what to expect and how to undertake it—and keep it simple. Some suggestions are to train at the same time of the day or the same days so that a routine is established, or being aware that it may be uncomfortable at times involved. We should keep notes on our program and progress as an incentive to keep going and to guide our improvement.
- We can learn about and understand ourselves, the sacrifices we are prepared to make and our willingness to stick to the action plan we have developed—we are the only one who can make the change and make

things happen, but through this there should be a real sense of achievement.

- We should examine our previous experiences with exercise, diets, etc. and whether there have been good and bad experiences that can be learnt from. We then look at why the previous experiences may not have been successful, and then look forward, not back as we don't want our past experiences to put us off our future achievements.
- We can ask ourselves where we would like to end up or be like so that a clear goal and direction can be established. This needs to be realistic so that it is achievable, making failure to achieve less likely.
- Be aware that with consistency, a sensible plan and a goal anything is achievable. It is the desire to want to change, coupled with a sensible and proven strategy and program that will help you achieve what you want.
- Any 'pain' involved in changing our way of life is far less than the 'pain and inconvenience' that will be experienced later in life through not undertaking some exercise program, and the longer the delay in reversing the effects of a sedentary life, the greater the effort (and 'pain') required to correct it.
- We should not expect change too quickly. As it may have taken years to reach our present condition, any improvement will take time—we look for improvements, no matter how small, and provide ourselves with little rewards along the way. We should praise ourselves when it is deserved.

Components of Fitness and Health

I see health and fitness having four components:

1. Strength;
2. Cardio-vascular fitness;
3. Nutrition; and
4. Flexibility.

If we can cover these components then we are on our way to a healthy, more energetic lifestyle. I will briefly talk about how strength and cardio-vascular fitness can be achieved. I have outlined some basic facts on nutrition and some hints on healthy eating. In terms of flexibility, I have not included any pictures in this book and it is difficult to describe a stretching routine. I would recommend a visit to a yoga class or similar (or purchase a book) to familiarise yourself with the most effective and safe way to stretch. I went to about five yoga classes, which was enough to learn a basic routine that I undertake most days at home. So while there is no detail in this book on flexibility, it is an important part of any fitness and health program and an activity that does not take much time. Most mornings I will spend 5-10 minutes stretching.

Strength Training

Why Strength Train

As people age there is a gradual but fairly consistent reduction in muscle size and muscle strength. As a general indication people over 21 years of age loose approximately 1 kg of muscle every 2-3 years. As people not exercising regularly invariably put on weight over time, this reduction in muscle is often hidden by the additional fat placed on the body. If we have, for example, put on 10 kg of weight over the last 10-15 years and have not undertaken any regular exercise or strength training, then we will have gained more than 10 kg of fat as fat weighs less than muscle and we will have experienced some muscle loss in that time.

Unless some form of weight bearing exercise is undertaken this muscle and strength loss will continue. Undertaking weight training with light weights will slow the progress of this loss, however over time some reduction will occur. In addition the results will be minimal and people tend to discontinue the program if the results are not visible.

Strength training is vital if we wish to become fit and healthy as muscle burns energy and is the key to the fat burning process. The larger the muscles the greater the energy burnt, even while resting and this usually continues for a reasonable period. The human body has been engineered for activity and we should encourage it to perform in this way. The benefits of exercise therefore last beyond the actual exercise session.

Muscle strength also assists in maintaining joint stability, improving posture and increases the capacity to undertake daily chores. It provides a boost to your energy levels and over time you will start feeling better about yourself. Undertaken consistently it will also enhance your appearance, particularly for men who want to gain bigger muscles. Women will not gain so much muscle as they have less testosterone. I have included a weight training program at the end of this book that I do every week. I have also provided a brief explanation of the way to train. Men and women have the basic functional anatomy and physiology in relation to their muscle and exercise response therefore what I have suggested works for both sexes, and these exercises are designed for both men and women.

Cardio-vascular Exercise

Many people undertake walking as a means of exercise and keeping fit. It is a great activity and is generally easier to do with your partner than harder exercise. Wendy and I enjoy walking together, the favourite place being along the beach or through some parks. As a family we ride our bicycles around the streets or cycle paths. We can talk without interruption and enjoy the outdoors as well as getting some exercise. We're fortunate that we live in a climate where year round outdoor activities is possible. Choosing a pleasant area to walk also helps you to walk further as it does not appear such a chore.

When exercising if we want to find out how hard we are exercising we can measure our heart rate per minute by taking our pulse rate for ten seconds and then multiplying it by six. We can do this during our exercise session. As a general indication our maximum heart rate is 220 minus your age (so for a 40 year old, it is 180). The maximum rate for a hard workout should be about 90-95% of this maximum (so about 170 beats per minute for a 40 year old).

When looking at starting an exercise program it is important that we choose something that we will enjoy as we are more likely to keep at it. I have given a couple of examples below that you wish to think about, but what you do depends on the time you have, whether you go to a gym, and whether it is easy to get outside and exercise (are you near a park or is it safe to walk along the streets). Taking up some formal exercise, perhaps in a team sports such as basketball or volleyball, always helps to motivate us as we don't want to let the team down by stopping. Training or exercising with someone also makes it easier as we can push each other along and therefore exercise harder.

We can all get more everyday exercise by not taking the car to work—perhaps ride our bicycle, take the lift up the building, or get off the bus a few stops before we would normally get off. Sometimes, we may know someone who lives close by who also works with us—we could walk or cycle to work with them.

Training on an Exercise Bike

An exercise bike can easily be placed inside the home or used in gyms. This type of equipment is especially useful if the weather is not good, you don't have a push bike or you simply don't like to get out on the streets on a bicycle. The following is an exercise that can be undertaken on this exercise bike—say an eight minute ride where you imagine going up a hill:

- Start with a warm up for about two minutes—relatively easy pace—try and keep at 75-80 revolutions of the pedals per minute.
- Increase the pace following the warm up by increasing the resistance on the bike and then start the climb by standing up to cycle—maintain 75-80 revolutions.
- Maintain this speed for two minutes and then sit down and adjust the resistance so that it is still at 75-80 revolutions.
- Remain seated for one minute but keep cycling—relax the shoulders.
- After one minute stand up again (adjusting the resistance again) and imagine climbing the hill attempting to pass

those in front of you—with this ride try and couple of harder pushes for about 10 secs each (making it harder by increasing the resistance but maintaining 75-80 revolutions).

- Sit down again and relax resistance to keep 75-80 revolutions and cycle for one minute.
- Stand up on the bike for one final push to the top of the hill.
- The above exercise can be repeated if you still have some energy and want to try and get fitter. Having some music on helps to keep us motivated.

If you live in an area that is flat and you like to get out on your bicycle for exercise then you could aim to ride approximately 100 metres as fast as you can or faster than you normally do, slow down for ten to fifteen seconds and then ride fast again. Repeat this as many times as you can.

Other Alternatives

If you have access to a pool, then running in the water is a great way to elevate the heart rate without stressing the joints. You also remain relatively cool throughout the session. This exercise can be done two ways:

- In shallow water where you can use your feet on the bottom of the pool and run as fast as you can keeping down low so that your arms are also in the water.
- Deep water running (where you cannot stand) can be achieved either with flotation belts or without, where you use the running as a form of treading water.

When to Exercise

Most people will have a particular time for training or exercising. The preference could depend on family, work, or lifestyle. If you feel comfortable exercising at a particular time and find it easier to keep with it, then great. If you are not sure when to train or exercise then the following are some ideas that you may wish to think about:

- Exercising first thing in the morning (before breakfast) provides a great start to the day, helps to keep your metabolism higher for the day and any remaining fat eaten from the previous day and night will be burnt off. When you have finished exercising, try and not have your breakfast for a while if possible (have a shower, stretch etc.). Once again, following exercise you will continue to burn the fat you ate from the previous day. Exercising first thing in the morning also means that it is out of the way, and you do not have to worry that something will come up later to prevent you from exercising.
- Exercise in the cool of the day. Exercising in the heat can stress the body and any bodyweight loss is mainly fluid anyway. You can also exercise harder when it is cooler.
- Do not exercise too late at night if it can be avoided (unless it is not too hard such as walking), as it can upset your sleeping pattern.
- If you have a family, time your exercise program with consideration to your family's needs so there are no conflicts or clashes that may make you feel guilty about taking up family time.

Finally, remember the importance of everyday movement. This movement is greatly underestimated as an important exercise. The reduction in this type of activity through such things as computers and television and sitting at an office desk all day is one reason the human race has become larger and more obese. As more people move to the cities their lifestyle changes—they get less physical exercise, they eat out more in fast food restaurants and they could more prepared meals rather than fresh food. Our bodies respond according to how we treat them. Do little and our bodies will start to get bigger and slower. Treat them right and we will get many miles out of them.

Nutrition (or Eating Our Way to Good Health)

Like exercise, nutrition plays an important part in our well-being. Our appearance, health, energy levels and our ability to undertake tasks or participate in activities (recreational or competitive) are all dependent on what we put into our mouth. Food and drink influence the way we feel. At the extreme we see children (and adults) who crave sugar as their bodies have become used to large doses—have a large lunch at work and we can become tired in the afternoon. Diabetes (particularly late-onset type 2) is becoming a major and more common health problem in both developed and developing countries and is partly a result of unhealthy eating. To many cultures, including India, their whole social arrangements and interactions are based around food. We usually invite friends or family around at breakfast, lunch or dinner time and we place great importance on preparing a great meal or snacks for the occasion.

Apart from keeping us alive the food fulfils a very important physical and social function. While playing an important part in our physical health, it can also be a problem. If we do not manage it properly it can have a devastating affect on our health and subsequently our relationship. Despite our best efforts over the last ten to twenty years (in terms of understanding nutrition, the introduction of low fat diets etc.) obesity and various lifestyle diseases have increased dramatically in many countries.

An exercise program and appropriate nutrition can result in weight loss or weight stabilisation. The trick is to consume only the food we need to expend energy—the more active we are the more food we will consume as our metabolism is consistently higher. A routine of regular exercise and regular eating means the body is always working to burn our food, which helps to regulate weight. We need to listen to our body and recognise its appetite and needs.

If we have a problem with our nutrition we need to examine our own eating actions, including the reason for our hunger. There are a number of issues that need to be considered for hunger and eating. These include:

- Our need to feed our body for the energy it has used. We have all experienced the symptoms of extreme hunger including dizziness, tiredness/weakness and not being able to concentrate.
- The satisfaction that we get from a meal, or food in general. Our love of food involves our five senses (touch, feel, sight, smell and sound)—many people cannot resist the smell of freshly baked bread, cakes or fried chips. Meals having an uninteresting texture often do not satisfy us and we go back looking for something more interesting (one reason that oily/fatty foods are easy to eat is because of the way they feel in our mouth).
- Eating a lot of food or starving ourselves can come from emotional problems. Food can assist us with problems in our lives, and if not fixed can become a health problem. In some cases food helps us shut out our emotions, particularly as it relates to anger, loneliness and jealousy.
- Food can also be a major source of pleasure or used to help us get over boredom. Often it means we will eat such foods as cakes, lollies or other unhealthy foods that contain high levels of fat and sugar. Sometimes, we may feel better emotionally as it has provided a distraction to our problems or we can end up feeling worse about ourselves as we realise we've eaten the food for the wrong reasons.
- Social occasions bring people together and we tend to eat more at these times.

It takes a big effort to overcome any eating difficulties. If we do have a problem we need to ask ourselves 'why am I eating'. That way we give ourselves time to think about why we are about to eat something unhealthy and whether it is for the right reasons—for example, is it because I am hungry, because I want to be distracted from a problem or because it will taste good?

We can then examine our eating habits in detail and look for any periods where we may have eaten something unhealthy, or more importantly where we have done so and it was not what we normally do. If it is on the odd occasion then generally we shouldn't be worried, however if it becomes a habit or appears to be out of control and we need to recognise that something should be done.

Nutritional Change in India

Religious and caste restrictions, weather, geography and the impact of foreigners determine the eating habits of Indians. There is no single cuisine in India. Just like the culture of India, the Indian cuisine is also very diverse. From Punjabi to South Indian to Gujarati, Indian food consists of a number of different regional cuisines. The staple diet of India consists of rice, atta (whole wheat flour), a variety of pulses and vegetables. Besides the main dishes, there are a number of snacks that are quite popular in India. Some of them are samosa, pakodas, vadas, chillas. The most popular drink is tea. Coffee is more popular in South India. Nimbu pani (lemonade), lassi, and coconut milk are also popular.

The traditional Indian diet has been high in calories, however more and more people are now eating out and eating more processed foods. The diets used to contain more fibre and grains, with many Indians vegetarians due to the prohibition of meat.

In 1993, a World Development Report showed an increase in the consumption of fat, saturated fat, sugar, salt and the clarified butter known as ghee. Even vegetarians are at risk as vegetarians in India tend to cook in fatty oils rather than eat them raw. In addition much of the population could not afford foods that were high in fat, processed foods or animal food products.

Dietary changes that have taken place as Indian populations move up the socio-economic scale appear to be:

- Increased intake of legumes, vegetables, milk (and flesh foods in case of non-vegetarians)—these changes are considered to be beneficial from the nutritional point of view.

- Substitution of coarse grains by the more refined cereals such as wheat and rice, with a preference for the highly polished varieties of the latter. This is also often accompanied by a reduction in the overall cereal intake.
- An increase in the intake of edible fat with increasing preference for saturated fat in place of vegetable oils and a high intake of *ghee* (clarified butter).
- Increased intake of sugar and sweets.
- Increase in overall energy intake in relation to energy expenditure, leading to obesity.

In many cases, the above changes are sufficient to cause an increase in diabetes and other lifestyle diseases.

With the increased Westernisation of India the food supply has increased, different foods have become available and Western style, commercial food has been introduced. With the increase in wealth of the Indian population people can also afford to eat out more often and have the Western style take-away. The Indian diet has therefore become less healthy as it moves towards high fat, high-energy (sugars) food. The use of high fat oils such as butter and plant oils and the reduction in eating rice, wheat products and vegetables has also contributed to the increase in a fatty diet.

This change is shown in the size of people. The problems associated with poor diet and increased obesity have an effect on relationships as they change lifestyle and contribute to early death. Overweight, unhealthy people have less energy, less self-discipline and as their bodies are not as fit they are often not seen as attractive to their partners or to themselves.

We need to educate ourselves that some things need to be eaten (the healthy things like fruit, vegetables and grain) and other things are unhealthy. We often have to be taught what is the right thing particularly as a society such as India changes and outside influences such as McDonalds and Pizza Hut come into the country. We are often not aware of the effects of eating too much of these foods until it is too late. As an Indian student describes:

> My dad's family was quite wealthy, and they ate a lot of meat. They also drank lots of fizzy drinks. They lived a "western" lifestyle. His brothers died at 33 and 45. Bowel cancer, heart disease, and diabetes affected all of them. My dad went into a diabetic coma and died when I was only 13 years old.
>
> My mom's side was poor, and they lived on one chicken a week, vegetables, fruit, and rice. My grandmother lived to 102 and my grandfather died at 88 of cancer. My mom is still very healthy.

We also need to make our children understand the differences between food that will keep them healthy and those will lead to health problems in the future. Explaining the differences between vegetables and cake is simple but a lot of them don't realise it.

Any improvements that we can bring to ourselves will help our relationship. Our decreased dependence on food (and drink) for example will help us become more productive and easier to get along with. Our partner will respect us more as we indicate that we value ourselves as we are trying to improve.

India initiated its process of developing dietary guidelines in 1997 and publicised the "Dietary Guidelines for Indians" in 1998. The guidelines were developed by the National Institute of Nutrition, Council on Medical Research, Ministry of Health and Family Welfare and reviewed by experts in nutrition, education paediatrics, and medicine. These guidelines suggested the following:

- Nutritionally adequate diet should be consumed through a choice of foods.
- Adequate and appropriate diet should be taken by children and adolescents, both in health and disease.
- Cooking oils and animal foods should be used in moderation, and vanaspati/ghee/butter should be used only sparingly.
- Over-eating should be avoided to prevent over-weight and obesity. Proper physical activity is essential to maintain desirable body weight.

- Highly refined and polished cereals should be avoided in preference to less refined cereals.
- Green leafy vegetables and fruits should be included as often as possible.
- Edible fat intake need not exceed 40 g and total fat intake can be limited to levels at which fat will provide no more than 20 per cent of the total energy.
- The intake of sugar and sweets should be restricted.
- High salt intake should be avoided.
- Water should be taken in adequate amounts and beverages should be consumed in moderation.
- Processed and ready-to-eat foods should be used judiciously.
- The elderly should eat a nutrient-rich diet to keep fit and active.

While also reducing our food intake there have been suggestions that a wider variety of foods consumed in our diet is also of benefit. Up to 30-40 different foods a week appear to be a healthy number (particularly low fat).

If we are serious about our diet and health then it is worth examining what we eat over a period of a week or so to discover the variety that we do consume.

General Principles/Tips

Due to educational programs and a growing understanding of the need to consume a healthy diet, people are generally aware of the rights and wrongs of eating and drinking. While acknowledging what I have written above concerning appropriate diet, I have outlined below some simple principles that I follow. They are simple to follow and can easily become a part of everyday life—there are no great sacrifices to face.

- Eat a low fat diet—sufficient fat can be obtained from eating a sensible low fat diet.
- Aim for a combination of 2/3 food, fruit and vegetables and 1/3 animal products (dairy, meat, poultry).
- It is important that a good breakfast is eaten.

- Do not have too many dairy products—to maintain calcium intake to retain bone density have small amounts of low fat milk, some cheese, small amounts of butter if necessary etc.).
- Drink plenty of fluids throughout the day, particularly water (2-3 litres minimum, and increase when exercising). We can use our urine colour as a guide. It is better if it is relatively clear rather than yellow, apart from our first morning urination.
- If we are going to have a work lunch or morning tea or are going out for dinner then we can have some food beforehand such fruit so that we will not eat so much, as people tend to eat more when socialising and the food eaten at these occasions is often high in fat and sugar.
- Watch alcohol intake as heavy drinking can help to put weight on. It is also not unusual for heavy drinkers to have poor diets and undertake little exercise.
- We can occasionally eat our favourite sweet or fattening 'food' such as chocolate—but we can try going for smaller portions of better quality than larger helpings of lesser quality. Why? In the long run it is just as cheap, less fattening and we may feel less guilt due to the smaller quantity involved. We will enjoy the experience and appreciate it more due to the better quality—life's too short to eat cheap chocolate.
- We can pick a day where we can eat a low fat healthy diet for that day. We can be creative and prepare and eat foods we have not had for a while (buy some unusual fruit, snack or dried fruit and nuts instead of sweets, have an omelette with different vegetables). Recipe books are great for getting ideas on spoiling ourselves while still eating healthy foods. This experience can introduce us to a greater range of both fresh and prepared foods, reducing any boredom that we may currently have with our diet that may mean we look at eating fast foods instead. This discipline for a

day can help us start an on-going healthy eating program.

- Consider balance, moderation and variety.

Placing the Emphasis on Ourselves

In addition to physical health discussed in this chapter, our mental/intellectual health can also suffer over time. By this I mean that once we have finished our formal education (whether it be high school or university), self-improvement can often stop, which can lead to mental staleness. And if there are no, or not many, interests outside of a relationship then partners can become bored (or one partner may become resentful if the other one is undertaking other interests).

We should consider pursuing a hobby or undertaking a course or an activity in an area that interests us, so that our brain remains active and fresh—we can try and find a passion for something. This helps us to maintain a certain amount of independence within our relationship so we are not dependent on our partner for stimulation, and we are also meeting our need for social interaction with other people. Once we start to feel comfortable in our relationship we can become lazy so that we stop growing, experimenting and trying new experiences. We need to be aware of what we are capable of, and care about pursuing and achieving some of the interests that we are going to find time to undertake.

Finding other interests can also be important if our job or career is not very exciting. As well as providing interest from our day-to-day living, it may help find us a different direction for a career change.

While it may be difficult to change our lifestyle immediately to achieve the benefits of a more positive life, it may be easier to start in one or two areas initially. Waiting for something to happen or to be presented to us will not work. It is no help knowing what to do without following up with some action. We can set some goals, plan them out and then check every so often on our progress. Trying to find what we really enjoy doing and writing it down is important. We are then able to look back at the end of the day and check whether there were things that made us feel good and those that did not.

While it is not always possible to avoid the difficult, the unpleasant or the inconvenient, it is essential that the things we have to do are balanced up with doing things that make us feel good. We have all felt the need to get away or to take a holiday where we can relax and do the things we want to do or things that we do not normally do but would love the time to do them. We may ask ourselves why we cannot fit anything more into our life and the answer is often 'I don't have the time to fit one more thing in'.

Sometimes people feel guilty about doing something for themselves. This is particularly the case where children are involved, where one partner dominates the relationship or women feel obligated to have children and stay at home.

Often Indian wives feel that there are rules in a marriage that they must respect at all cost. Some of these wives see themselves as less important than their husband and they put their needs after their husband's. They often try and make their husband happy before thinking about their own happiness. Some had even given up things they usually like to do because of their family commitments. This often happens when a person sees themselves not as an individual but as a family member only. Therefore, their fulfilment comes from the family rather than from their own achievements. While I strongly believe that family is the most important unit in society, it is important that family life is not all-consuming, so that all other interests and social contact are excluded. As a society such as India changes, this can lead to dissatisfaction in people's lives as they are not achieving something themselves, particularly if others around are achieving.

However, with the changes occurring in Indian society, more and more people are now able to have more choices so that they can satisfy themselves more and are taking advantage of this to create their own lives as they would like. An Indian teacher and her husband have been married for four years. They intend not to have any children:

> Marriage and motherhood are no longer obligations for women to undertake. Indian society is now more tolerant to people having their own choices and we are quite happy not to have children.

Women actively participate not only in their family affairs, but also in social and political activities in the community. Many younger people are surfing the net for information. A survey showed that of those interviewed, 51% had been involved in training courses to increase their skill levels. Many of these hoped to travel overseas within the next five years. Young women who have moved away from home and are working in factories or offices or starting their own businesses are gaining in confidence. They are finding their own individual worth and their own potential. This self-worth needs to be kept, even when entering a relationship or marriage.

We have three children and they take up a lot of time. If it is not running them from one activity to another (and I believe that many children take part in too many structured activities for their own and parents' good) then it's checking homework. Children know what they want and in all likelihood will ask for it. At all ages they appear to have little concept of being selfish or uncaring despite constant reminders that they are not the only people on the earth.

We love our kids, have a great relationship with them and we spend great times with them. However, we are careful that we do not just act out of duty or obligation at all times as that soon leads to resentment for both our own role and towards our children—we also expect some giving from our children as well:

> It is especially important that children have even more experiences outside the home in order to learn different ways of socializing and cooperating with others. It is important that the child is not constantly in the company of one or both parents as there are many activities that they can participate in. This will help the child to understand the world more as well as giving the parents the break they sometimes need from their children.

We do need and want time to ourselves (Wendy and I together) as well as individually. We should not have to or be expected to say yes to everything. Having our own mind indicates a respect for ourselves. We should value our ability to make a decision that may not always please somebody else and which does not leave you feeling uncaring. We can try it next time we feel unsure between what we believe is right for us and what other people expect from us. As we become more comfortable with saying no to demands and requests for our time, where appropriate, we will discover that we are considerate with other people where and when it counts. We start to feel better about ourselves, which can only improve our relationship with our partner and those around us.

The point here is that we can get so involved in our existing lifestyle that there does not appear to be any spare time to fit those extra little activities that mean something to us. People who plan their lives give themselves a greater opportunity for being happier than those who stumble through bored and with no direction. Planning is the key to taking responsibility for ourselves. I have expanded on this point in the habit dealing with balancing your lifestyle with some ideas on leading a more proactive life.

A friend of mine finds it difficult to complete tasks. This person often has two or three jobs to do and instead of completing one and then moving on, she is trying to finish all three. It is frustrating to her and her husband as none of the jobs get done in a reasonable time, she gets depressed and angry and the relationship suffers. She knows what she'd like to do but can't seem to get around to doing it.

We can try to focus so we have less chance of ending up in this situation—as mentioned earlier, this may mean saying no to demands from other people. We learn to finish particular jobs and we can move on quite comfortably to other tasks—we are then able to see our way to things you would like to do. And if we can see that our partner needs that time to themselves to complete whatever it is they are working on, then we should provide that space or help out with the rest of the family so they have some peace and time to themselves. We could all learn to better recognise and understand when our partner is under pressure or needs that break to recover.

Wendy and I recently had a night away in a hotel for our twentieth wedding anniversary. We had lunch out, lazed around the pool, dressed up and went out for dinner, had a few drinks late into the night, slept in and went to breakfast at a café. Most of the time we just talked. We didn't worry about the time or our children (they had $20 to spend on pizza for dinner so they were happy to be home by themselves). While it was only a short time away we both found it very refreshing and very romantic and we still felt great weeks later—it's an experience that we have remembered as we went back into our day-to-day routine. If you do have a little spare money why not think about having a night away in a nice hotel where you can enjoy the facilities in the hotel—enjoy the luxury of the room, get dressed up and go to a nice restaurant, drink in the hotel bar, make good use of the big, freshly made bed.

If we can see our way to providing more time for ourselves as well as appreciating this need in our partners then our relationship becomes far more enjoyable.

Building Confidence in Ourselves

Confidence is how we feel about ourselves and how we relate to the world and allows us to set goals and to lift our hopes and expectations. Setting goals and leading a proactive life is covered in more detail in the last habit relating to balancing your lifestyle.

In this section I am going to suggest that in order to build confidence in our partner we first need to start with ourselves. If we don't feel good about ourselves, doubt we have the ability to undertake challenges, or feel that we don't deserve much from our partner then we could be lacking confidence. If we are lacking inner confidence then it will be very difficult to give confidence to our partner because we do not know what it feels like. We may find it difficult to show that we believe in our partner if our own self-respect is low, to give honest feedback or to take the right action if we lack confidence. Alternatively, we may also try and please our partner in attempt to show our worth—a confidence booster to ourselves. All of this can cause confusion in a relationship as we try to work out our own thoughts—our understanding of our partner can then be more difficult. There may be a number of reasons why we may lack confidence, including:

- A lifetime of being told that we are not worth much or loved, particularly from people we respect.
- Previous relationship problems.
- Being picked on or bullied at school.
- Some kind of incident that reduces our confidence.
- General low esteem caused by depression.

These tend to indicate that our confidence level is a result of an unhappy experience or upbringing—we can be a victim of what has happened in the past. To improve our confidence we can try the following:

General Changes

- We can be aware of and acknowledge when we are succeeding—we look at things, no matter how small, that we have done well. It may have been some work around the house or success in our job or business.
- Instead of saying we cannot do something, we change it around and look at how we can do it. We can read about it, ask someone with experience or undertake a course. And often the only way we'll learn is by making mistakes. I've never undertaken a writing course and the thought of competing with professionally trained writers, counsellors and the like was not easy. To learn about a different society and culture such as India's has been an exciting experience for me.
- We keep positive during setbacks so that our confidence does not disappear. We try to not be too hard on ourselves as we experience life. Not everything will go our way—sometimes it is a result of things outside of our control anyway.
- If we believe that there is some past experience or incident that is affecting our ability to fully participate

in and enjoy life then we may need to seek counselling. It can often take a great deal of talking to reach a problem that we have not been aware of. This may require us to talk to a counsellor and identify all the possible problems.

- We should not compare ourselves with others as we all have strengths and weaknesses. Unless we're the best in the world at something (and that is often short-lived) we should not try to compete. We do or look the best we can or desire and expect no more. If we go to the gym twice a week to achieve a certain level of fitness and health we shouldn't expect to look the same as a person who spends five days there—but we may have a better balanced life.

Specific Changes

Hopefully as we start to feel better on the inside it will also affect our outward manner or appearance. I have covered some of this in the earlier part of this chapter, but consider the following:

- Walk strong and confidently. Our posture will give a lot away as well as influencing how we feel. I was watching a game of soccer last weekend and I could tell who was winning. The team not winning had their head and shoulders forward and down, no spring in their steps, and there was no communication between the players. That was in the space of about twenty minutes of football—imagine a long period of time where we have been depressed or had problems.
- We should make the effort to look good. We can look at doing what we can and does not require anything major such as cosmetic surgery or extreme diets. Wendy used to work behind the counter in a swimming pool shop, where she tested pool water and sold chemicals. She usually wore shorts and a T-shirt. While that dress was appropriate for what she was doing, Wendy loved to dress up on other occasions. She looked great and it made her feel good. She wears

clothes that flatter her and she takes pride in how she does look. And she knows how I feel about the effort she makes and how good she looks. We should dress well when we go out and make an effort with the rest of our appearance. Dress and present yourself for the occasion.

- While remembering the last point, we need to be aware that within a short time after people meet with us our physical appearance will not be as important as our personality—'good looks catch the eye, but a good personality catches the heart'. We should try to be natural and positive, and be confident in how we present ourselves. In a larger group we can include ourselves in any discussion; we should speak up and share our thoughts. This becomes easier if we undertake some self-education such as reading the paper, watching current affairs/news or documentaries. That may sound boring but the world is an interesting place and we can find out what is happening in other places. As India becomes more international there is a greater opportunity for you to learn about, and perhaps see, what is going on in other countries. Having a passion or interest can make us an expert or an authority on something, where we can educate or teach other people—I find a great satisfaction in passing on my fitness and health knowledge.
- We can think about what we are capable of doing. This could mean setting ourselves a new challenge or new targets. I'm in a fairly strict routine with my exercise program. However, I am still looking at improvements, perhaps different ways of doing things that can challenge my body further. Wendy commenced a new job a couple of years ago. While some of the work was similar to what she has done in the past, her manager has gradually passed on more responsibilities and a greater variety as Wendy has shown a capacity and interest in taking on more and a willingness to

challenge herself, to the extent that the people in the office really depend on her.

Hopefully the above will help you feeling more positive about yourself. Having a look at ourselves does not necessarily mean that we do lack confidence. However, there may be some areas that we can improve on. We can picture ourselves as we work through the above list and see if it makes a difference to our confidence. A confident person brings life and understanding to a relationship.

Self-respect

Self-respect, as opposed to self-esteem, comes about from our concern for others and living our own lives according to our principles and ideals. It is gained through the hard slog of life and accommodates failure and disappointments and our responses to these experiences. Self-esteem on the other hand generally means that we should be striving to be happy, recognised for our achievements and we should be looking for ways to be feeling good about ourselves. While it is nice to be told that we are wonderful and be praised for any little achievement it is often short-lived and we then go looking for the next piece of good news to lift us again. Self-respect however acknowledges failure as a part of life, but we continue to like ourselves despite this as we look to overcome and learn from failure and move on. We can draw strength from the fact that we have overcome any hurdles.

This self-respect does not depend on success because there are always failures to contend with. Neither is it a result of comparing ourselves with others because there is always someone better. Comparisons and the seeking of rewards or encouragement are often the tactics used to increase our self-esteem. With self-respect, we simply like ourselves or we don't. With self-esteem, we like ourselves because of who we are and not because of what we can or cannot do. So while I appreciate any compliments I may receive regarding this book, my real feeling of accomplishment comes from the discipline in sitting down and researching, thinking and writing, my sense of achievement in completing the work and the satisfaction that may come from at least one person reading it and learning something.

Self-respect is about making promises to ourselves and living those promises on a daily basis. When I decide to make changes in my life, I decided to increase my well-being on all levels. This included more creativity, financial and business success, improved relationships and a healthy life.

In some cases I have had to make large changes in letting go of things that slowed or prevented my success. Once I was able to put various things into place, the easier it all became. As my self-confidence and self-respect grew, I have been able to deal with any obstacles in my way.

As a confident person you will generally not settle for second best and you should have some idea of what you want out of the relationship. Confident people (and I mean those who are comfortable in themselves as opposed to those who appear to give off a type of brash confidence that is similar to arrogance and vanity) are more likely to put the effort into listening to and understanding their partner—they will be more in touch with themselves and this often translates to a recognition of their partner's need. You will look for success as you know how to find it and you know what it feels like. Perhaps each of you can draw up a list of what you need and want in your relationship and see how it matches.

Confident partners are more likely to have give and take in a relationship. Having self-respect will signal that you have something to offer each other, while also being special enough to receive something in return.

Having little self-respect can cause real problems in relationships and friendships. It's a problem that is often self-perpetuating as depression sets in which further reduces self-respect as your opinion of yourself is poor. Positive experiences that would normally provide you with that little boost become few and far between. Your own relationship doesn't excite you—any positives that may come out of it may give you temporary relief, however your mindset is such that any problems will outweigh the good. Depression is difficult to overcome and professional help is often required.

In general terms consider the following as a test as to whether you have self-respect or not:

- Little self-respect—an over-reliance on what you are doing in the present as a guide to how you feel about yourself—basically you often question your self-worth and abilities. Your personal satisfaction level is usually dependent on external factors, and these are often short-lived. Bad experiences and problems are often seen as long-term and can be all consuming. For example, how you are treated, your successes or failures, and meeting your own standards which may be too high. Negative thinking tends to be ingrained into the human psyche and many people tend to remember the failures more than the successes that they may have. When life is running smoothly, how often do we acknowledge that things are good? It is often when there is a problem that we take notice of where we are at and we then dwell on these hiccups or past failures. These negative emotions tend to be more long-lasting, whereas moments of joy and happiness appear to be more short-term and can be used as a means for shoring up our self-respect (for many people happiness can mean shopping—retail therapy, a pay rise and other such distractions).
- Self-respect—you know yourself well and accept what you are unconditionally. You recognise and acknowledge your strengths, virtues and weaknesses—this allows you to think, act and feel in a far more positive way. Having self-respect often results from participating in meaningful activities and involving ourselves with good friends and in relationships that mean something—we become absorbed in our activities. We may desire the material things such as a wider screen television or an expensive mobile phone, however we often get tired of these very quickly as they can often be just a status symbol. Having self-respect

means we learn to saviour those experiences that really mean something and we engage in both relationships and activities that will boost the positive emotions. We avoid looking for the short-term thrills. We also focus more on the positives and acknowledge that in most cases problems are short-lived and within our control.

We can try the following if our self-respect is low:

- Be good to ourselves—we can think about our positive points and use those to inspire us to do other things.
- We should not depend on other people to make us feel good—we learn to depend on ourselves. We take control by making our own decisions and then enjoying any accomplishments. If someone is not enthusiastic about our achievements then learn to ignore the way they feel as our own thoughts count.
- We should not always try and set too higher a standard—if we keep failing our self-respect can suffer.
- We can appreciate ourselves, rather than trying to compare and compete against others.
- We enjoy what we achieve, rather than trying to please other people. We can then feel more comfortable doing what we want and we feel more in control.
- Acknowledge that there will be experiences of disappointment, deprivation and times when we fail. These are the times when we can grow.
- We seek, or have found, meaningful work and projects, and that is the source of our happiness.
- We continue to look for our needs, wishes, values and we try and live in in accord with them.
- While we look after ourselves and our appearance, we do not dependent on it for our self-image.

The only person who can initiate any change to your self-respect is yourself. You have to be willing to change and move forward—hopefully this book has provided some guidance in this area.

A great relationship allows, or helps, you and your partner to grow and to become the person you both want to be. You will then look forward to and appreciate the time spent together—a strong friendship develops in the relationship.

Believe in Yourself

...and in your dream
though impossible things may seem,
someday, somehow you'll get through
to the goal you have in view.

Mountains fall and seas divide
Before the one who in his stride
Takes a hard road day by day,
Sweeping obstacles away.

Believe in yourself and in your plan,
Say not—I cannot—but, I can.
The prizes of life we fail to win
Because we doubt the power within.

Spend Time with Your Partner, Talk with Them—Become Their Best Friend

7

A strong basis for any good relationship is friendship. Good friends are able to talk about anything and enjoy each other's company. I have observed relationships, however, where both partners would rather spend time with their friends, rather than with their partners. With videos, computers, work and the general busy lifestyle that people live these days, conversation between partners has tended to become less and less. They have time for everything and everyone but each other.

Men are traditionally considered goal-oriented and often their approach to situations are black and white—that is straight forward. Men, as opposed to women, use as little words as possible. I know with my male friends the conversation is often superficial and lacking the emotion or detail that my women friends exhibit. Men tend to be more cautious in what they say and their words that they do use reveal very little about their feelings toward the subject or the person they are speaking to. It is a characteristic of men that their intimacy is not so much in their communication but in undertaking a shared activity with their partner. Men are often sensitive to their partner's needs, however the way they communicate it sometimes makes it difficult for their partner to understand and respond to what they are saying.

Communication

Keep talking and listening. A lack of information passing between partners and the reduction of communication on a more personal level required to keep a relationship alive leads to misunderstandings and a growing distance between partners.

This can happen slowly to us over time so that neither partner notices the lack of time spent together until perhaps one incident leads to a major problem—in some cases however little disagreements with each other are a good indication that not enough time is being spent together, and that there are serious problems, resentments and anger occurring in the relationship.

Disagreements or differences of opinion are not necessarily unhealthy and can provide stimulation to a relationship. It is how they are resolved or discussed and how long they go on for that is important—we need to be aware of the emotions that exist in a relationship, otherwise attempts to find solutions or offer an opinion on something may not help. Emotional or abusive language will affect both partners' abilities to express themselves clearly and greatly affects the flow of conversation between partners. We should listen to ourselves speak—our tone, words used and our ability to talk about things that really matter in the relationship—and see how what you are saying may affect our partner. We may have different ways of saying things to our partner and it makes it easier if we recognise and accept that there will be differences, particularly if we are both being honest and considerate of each other—a certain amount of misunderstanding sometimes is normal, but we need to try and understand what our partner is saying.

Wives often just want a husband who can sit down and listen and someone who can appreciate her emotions. Husbands often want to reason with or perhaps just lecture their partner. Wives then often feel they are talking to a brick wall and may eventually stop sharing their thoughts and feelings. Keeping secrets kills passion in a relationship.

When I have a problem that I cannot solve on my own I will generally go to Wendy and say "Can I ask your advice?" I have discovered with Wendy that if I tell her about the problem in a matter of fact way then that is her cue to offer a solution. But with many men however, if they are advised of a problem then they will automatically go into a "fix it" mode and tell their partner exactly what they should be doing to resolve the problem. This is where yet another breakdown in communication begins.

To maintain a healthy relationship it is important that we learn to communicate our feelings with affection and warmth. Even fairly innocent statements or comments have the potential to cause conflict if they're said as commands, in an angry voice or in insulting language—our partner may respond as though we are making a personal attack on them and the problem then becomes bigger.

While we are in a conversation or especially a disagreement we often listen to bits and pieces of what our partner has to say. We are busy forming in our own minds what it is that we want to say next rather than really hearing what is being said to us. Misunderstanding the conversation and jumping to conclusions is very easy because we have only heard the key words that were spoken. Wendy and I practice actually listening to each other—it is easy to concentrate on the words being said as we are then not thinking of the next thing to say. It may take Wendy and I a little longer to respond to each other, however we have only considered our reply when the other has finished—don't be in a hurry to move the conversation to your side of things.

I read about the experience of an unhappy Indian family that was having trouble with their son who was not doing well at school. He was lazy and did not pay attention. The mother took responsibility for trying to get him to work harder and do his homework. However, the mother would kick and scream at her son and call him names. She was uneducated and therefore could not really help the son in his homework, but continued to get angry with him. The son also yelled back, but then would laugh and joke—he didn't seem to care. The boy's father would sit in the bedroom/living room listening to what was going on but not willing to help out or take part in the discussion. The father did regret not helping out with trying to help his son, however he blamed it on his own work and being tired. The television was switched on at dinner time and this provided a short-term break from the fighting and arguing that was going on in the household and the three of them watched television instead of talking.

Suggestions for the family to take a walk together in the evening to escape the anger in the house were usually greeted with the excuse that there was not time and the son needed to study. The concerns of the parents were understandable as their son probably would not go to university because of his low marks. However, the way that the problem was treated made the problem worse. The parents were advised about providing confidence in their son, reinforcing and highlighting any good things that occurred, and encouraging each other in their day-to-day life. These methods were tried for a short while, however the mother went back to her ways of hitting and abusing her son and checking his homework even more carefully. The father still ignored the problem.

With India's push into the more developed world, problems such as the above may have to be addressed. There is that competition to succeed, a blend of the old traditional ways that compete with Western culture. The West has had many years to try and deal with the sort of problem, sometimes without success. Indian families are grappling with these issues without a lot of experience and not much guidance.

Indian wives can still be constrained in their marriage even as Indian society is changing. They will often put their needs after their husbands and look at trying to keep their husbands happy and their family together. However, this can come at a cost as the quote below shows:

> I try and not disturb my husband in the morning. I put up with his temper so that he feels attached to me and there is peace in the family. I won't talk back to him if he becomes annoyed with me particularly in public as I give face to him.

Sacrifice and trying to keep their husbands happy can be a concern for Indian wives, particularly if their husbands do have a temper and use anger as a way of communicating.

As more Indian marriages are entered into because partners love and care for each other rather than through the traditional arranged marriage, it is important that areas of conflict are dealt with so that the relationship does not become stressed. Communication skills and the importance of harmony within the family needs to be recognised so that each partner understands what their partner is thinking. As one couple stated:

> My wife seemed to want sexual intimacy everyday, however I was not interested or do not have the desire for it. I did not speak to my wife about it but it made me unhappy. When it became a big problem we sought help and the doctor advised us to talk about it and I realised that my wife did not want sex everyday. We have now reached an agreement and we are able to talk about this subject much more openly.

As well there is the possibility of conflict as Indian couples pursue their careers, studies and so on as the economy rapidly expands and people can see that they can better themselves. This can cause one or both partners to be absent from the relationship as well as conflict within each person as they pursue their own interest, perhaps at the expense of the relationship.

> 'I am finding that I am spending more time at my work as everyone else is, and I don't want to be seen as lazy, said a Mumbai office worker. My work colleagues will also have a better chance of moving ahead in the company as they work harder. My wife does not like the time I spend away, and we fight about it at home. I try and explain it but she does not seem to understand.'

We are sometimes forced to confront a partner who may be angry or upset and we have trouble knowing how to respond or understanding what our partner means. Should we put up with an angry partner so as to keep the peace or should we assert ourselves and consider our own individual freedom?

In many societies the husband's power can contribute to the emotional distance between him and the rest of the family, particularly if this power comes from his position in a company. Because of this, his wife and children know that he may become firm or demanding, in which case they become cautious, reserved and find it hard to be completely at ease in his presence. This cautiousness makes communication difficult as family members are hesitant to speak through fear of upsetting their father or husband. It is important we each examine what our level of communication is in our relationship. Is it easy, free flowing, free of argument and enjoyable? Our family is one where free speech is encouraged and where all members can express their own ideas in a friendly atmosphere. Abusive language and personal attacks are not allowed.

Often it is how people approach the problem that is really the problem in itself—they could become angry, hit out or just sit there and not do anything. It is therefore important that if we are not happy about a particular incident that, in giving a clear message, we describe how we are actually feeling about something. Instead of 'you always...you never...' try 'when you do such and such, I feel...'. This puts the onus on our feelings rather than attacking our partner, and our partner will hopefully respond to this. We do not need to call our partner (or children) names as that will immediate upset them and they will then become defensive and will not listen to what we are trying to say. Our partner has a much clearer understanding of how a particular action has affected us—there is nothing wrong with being honest with our feelings if our partner has upset us. We have the right to express our feelings while our partner has the right to expect a clear indication from us on how we feel about something.

We should try and solve issues/problems when we are both relaxed and more likely to listen to alternative ideas and suggestions—we can see it as an exchange of views. We should learn the difference between significant and insignificant problems or issues and give them due consideration. In raising an issue/problem that may have been worrying us for a while it is sometimes better to start with a question. For example 'can we talk about...?, rather than 'I would like to talk about...'. While the end result may be the same, using the first example offers the follow advantages:

- It gives our partner some choice as to whether they wish to talk.
- It indicates to our partner that if it is not a good time to talk they have an opportunity to discuss it another time.

- The use of 'we' means that both partners are involved and we are not putting the blame on our partner.
- It is a softer approach, particularly if it is a sensitive topic.

Conversations in our relationship do not always have to be 'world problem' solving ones. We do not need to wait until we have something important to say or information to pass on—something as simple as talking about our day, who we saw, what they said, keeps us both involved. Talking is a great way to maintain and keep the relationship healthy and helps the emotional intimacy in it. Women are especially good at this and as a result they are often able to maintain more close friendships, particularly with girl friends outside of a relationship than men. There will be times where family and financial issues, for example, require discussion, however Wendy and I will often have days where we spend most of our time laughing at things said—it's great for the relationship, and we are prepared not to take ourselves too seriously. A relationship containing fun and excitement will be a far more relaxing one and tensions are less likely to arise. It is important that we find things to laugh about and we can share these moments with our partner. Share a joke, hire a funny movie, or laugh together about something that happened at work.

If lifestyle (long work hours and other commitments, etc.), results in limited time with our partner then it is important that time be set aside where both of us can just talk or participate in an activity together. Activities as simple as taking a walk in the park, a bicycle ride, playing a game or sport together or taking in a movie regularly are easily achievable. Finding something we both enjoy doing together is important as it is very relaxing and our time together and our relationship will benefit. Wendy and I work in the same town and we will often have coffee together at lunch time. Without children, television and other good and bad distractions it is nice to be able to sit and talk about whatever comes into our head. It could be what happened at work that morning, something we have read or, just talking about our children. It is not always possible to openly discuss issues about our children because, as they get older, they are more likely to be around us rather than in bed. Perhaps you may live in a small unit where it is difficult to talk without them hearing. Always be on the lookout for new things to talk about.

It's easy to fall into the routine of all work and no play, especially after children are born and careers begin to get more demanding. We need to make sure to take time to have fun together. Play time recharges our batteries and improves our moods. When we do it together as a family we all benefit.

Technology was supposed to make things easier for society as a whole. Indians, like elsewhere, are experiencing more and more technology in their lives. It has allowed many jobs and tasks to be made easier. However, with e-mail, the Internet and mobile phones/SMS, communication has taken on an entirely different face to what it was ten to fifteen years ago. We SMS or go into chat rooms to communicate and often the conversations tend to be short, to the point and lacking emotion. We then all get involved in the Internet and mobile phone craze, and this trend is also having an effect on relationships, particularly dating. Text messaging and Internet chatting is allowing those people who are perhaps shy to conduct a relationship without the fear of face-to-face talking. However, this should not be instead of the more meaningful relationship that is conducted when people are actually talking face-to-face. Communication between partners is probably the most important component of a good relationship and can only be learnt at this personal level.

Television and computers are also partly to blame for the rising obesity rate of the general population particularly children and, television in particular, can prevent conversation. This new technology can prevent us having meaningfully and effective communication. It makes us lazy as it is easier to sit and watch television and comment on what is happening on the television than it is to sit there and have a conversation with our partner.

> My husband used to say to me, 'You have a good job we have a roof over our head, what more do you want', said Sudhir, who divorced her husband a couple of years ago. She said, 'I wanted a husband who didn't sit home all day, watching sports on the television.'

I also remember when personal computers on everyone's desk were first introduced into the work place followed by the introduction of e-mail. Instead of coming into work, looking around, perhaps having a conversation with your work colleagues, the first thing many people do is switch on their computer and stare at the screen—scrolling through the interesting e-mails is what everyone does. Rather than walk downstairs to deliver a message to a work colleague it is e-mailed, perhaps saving two minutes and your legs don't get any exercise.

As this technology has been introduced over a number of years people become used to it, forgetting how it was ten years ago and perhaps not realising the impact it can have on relationships if the effort is not made to make-up for any lose in direct communication with our partner.

Remember the rule that we can talk about anything with our partner—life and death, family, work, holidays, children and so on. It does not matter what we talk about. What is more important is what we say and how we say it. The subject is not important as we increase our knowledge and learn to communicate with our partner more fully through conversation. We learn to form an opinion on something.

Don't Take Our Partner for Granted

Wendy and I been married 21 years and we have a great relationship. But we try not to take it the relationship or each other for granted. We both try to feel secure enough in ourselves that we're not looking to the other one for all of our needs. We both know that we can't always use our own values as a guide to understanding how the other person will react. I need to ask Wendy sometimes and she asks me . And I do not always know what Wendy needs or wants, so I ask and she tells me. When we can both talk about why something is important to us, it's always easier to find a way forward, particularly if there is a problem to solve.

One thing neither of us expects is that improvements or solutions have to be reached right away. We recognise that we both need to feel safe and accepted. I believe that problems start and continue when we forget what our partner is a thinking, and feeling.

A friend of mine described to me a few years ago about her marriage that she had been in for a length of time. She described it as comfortable. Knowing them I understood that to mean that the marriage was reasonably happy, but not great—the excitement had gone out of it. That is one of the biggest dangers in a relationship—taking each other for granted, where there is little excitement left and the relationship just leaves you feeling only comfortable. It is a little like being in a job for too long and the excitement and learning has stopped. There are now a greater number of people in India who have that higher expectation of love and marriage and are less willing to overlook the problems. While marriages may appear to be stable there may also be low quality and it is important that factors that contribute to a low quality marriage are identified.

In fact marriages can become pretty ordinary. Boredom can be a real conversation killer in a relationship as partners basically run out of things to say. We get to know each other pretty well in a relationship and if there is no continuing stimulation then we can become stale with each other through this familiarity. As mentioned, television, computers and the like can become the substitute for conversation and entertainment as we stop connecting with our partner and we become very lazy. Frustrations will very quickly creep into a relationship if one partner is bored. A partner who is not interested in the relationship, the one who goes off and sits in front of the computer or the television, will not respond to our needs and requests and the conversations tend to be from one partner only.

I have mentioned some ideas for improving ourselves in other chapters, including developing interests and expanding our knowledge on issues of interest—developing a passion for something. While we may be improving ourselves it takes two to do that in a relationship. We may need to consider or find ways to inspire our partner if they are not interested in participating in anything meaningful—simple encouragement and support can get our partner going.

A friend of ours died a few months ago. He was only 27 years old and his death, while not totally unexpected, was sudden. Wendy went to his funeral and apart from the service itself the most distressing sight was the man's widow following the hearse to the cemetery. We both spoke about this incident and the fact that this would be the last time that our friend would be in her husband's company.

We also realised how this type of event makes us think about our own life. The death of this man at such a young age reinforced my relationship with Wendy. What if that funeral had been Wendy's? It's times like those that I think about the twenty-five years we have known each other and the twenty-one years we have been married. I remember all the good times, the places visited, the three children we have raised together and the future that we have. We both talk about how we are going to grow old together and what we plan to do. Try that with your partner and imagine life without your partner—their smile, their laugh, the smell of their skin and hair, their companionship, and you may realise what they really mean to you or it reminds you what you already knew.

Some people may see being in a relationship as affecting their general freedom, how much money they don't have because of it, the freedom to pursue other relationships or not being able to concentrate on their careers. We often forget about the time and effort required in finding a suitable partner, going through dating and then in many cases finding the relationship is not working and moving on—it can be a pretty unhappy process, particularly if one or both partners have also been badly hurt in a previous relationship.

So be grateful for what you do have rather than some dream that there is someone better out there—and if you did find someone would they necessarily match up to your current partner. Studies indicate that second marriages have a greater chance of failing than first ones. For one, they can bring problems with them, but there arc other reasons, so make the first one count. Boredom within a relationship can lead to affairs as people seek more excitement.

> A married couple in Delhi both work and have good jobs. However, the husband has the opportunity to take on extra work as he gets a promotion. His wife finally has to give up her job as she has been trying to juggle her work, looking after a child and doing the housework. While she is happy with her husband's success, she starts to become bored with her life at home and becomes suspicious of her husband—she thinks he is having an affair. The husband is put off by his wife's behaviour and is attracted to someone else. Eventually the marriage breaks down and they divorce.

The important issues here are the boredom in the marriage which then leads to the wife not trusting her husband. The husband then seeks to escape from this by seeing another woman.

Trusting your partner becomes a very important issue as well as the ability to keep a marriage interesting.

Trust

Trust is one of the most important parts of a relationship. It provides the all-important security for partners. We have all probably been let down some time in our lives by someone we know, whether it is someone in a personal relationship or a work colleague. It can be devastating if that trust has been broken, particularly if that person is close. That trust, once broken is very difficult to repair.

However, not trusting someone means that we do not have full confidence in them and we are then often hesitant about having a relationship with them. It can limit our relationship in that we are always suspicious of them and it can affect the way we are with them. This can quickly lead to a total breakdown in trust. Trusting each other allows us both to confidently attempt new experiences and conduct ourselves in different ways. This can only improve the quality of our relationship as it gives us both the freedom to act without the need to justify or explain what we are doing.

I have undertaken a massage course and massaged only females and been involved in a marketing business involving visiting people in the homes after hours—it has never been a problem from Wendy's side as she trusts that I will not have an affair. This is not a case of having earned Wendy's trust as I do not believe you should have to earn such a thing in a relationship. In our marriage our actions speak for themselves. We have both established a trust through our actions. In other words, do our actions and commitments to date indicate that we can be trusted. It only takes one, perhaps two, instances where if this trust were broken a relationship starts to go bad. The more serious the breaking of the trust, such as an affair, the greater the betrayal and apart from the hurt, the question then is 'are you fully committed to the relationship'.

Violence by men in marriages is often because they believe there partner is having an affair—the trust is not there anymore. The sharp rise in extra-marital affairs in India indicates that with the greater freedom that has occurred in the country has also lead to breaches of trust within marriages. There are of course many reasons why these affairs may be taking place and I have mentioned some reasons already in this book and some possible solutions to helping the relationship before it reaches this stage. Having an affair is a great breach of trust and it is hoped that the relationship can be saved before it reaches this level.

You may be aware of relationships where one partner, and sometimes both, makes it very difficult for the other to undertake activities that may involve meeting with the opposite sex, for fear, for example, that it may lead to an affair. Where one partner is involved with the other sex whether it be with work, social or sport can lead to jealousy on the part of the other partner. This becomes more common in a country such as India in which its citizens are experiencing for the first time greater freedom and more opportunities to mix with people of the other sex.

One of the major reasons for male violence on a partner is because of this jealousy. A general lack of trust has led to many cases where the relationship has ended because of the control by one partner over the other. Our lives rely on relationships and social contacts that exist with other people, and the quality, extent and trust in forming and continuing these experiences is vital if we are to experience a quality of life, as opposed to an isolated one where we sit at home and do nothing for fear of what our partner may say. In terms of contentment, a life that is social and full of interaction with other people has a far greater chance of being a happy one than one that is spent alone. This alone makes for a happier relationship.

A good starting point is whether we trust ourselves—that is essential. You cannot change the other person in your relationship, so the best place to start is yourself. Consider the following situation:

> You work for a company and it sends you away to another big city for two nights for training. You go out for a walk and then return to your hotel. You obtain your room key and walk up to your room. You unlock the door and walk into the room only to find the company's gorgeous local secretary (or very handsome and rich manager) lying naked on your bed with a mischievous smile on her/his face. What is are you to do—do you trust yourself to look away while the person dresses and then ask them to leave or, being alone in a city away from your partner with a person you will never see again, do you succumb to your desires.

In India there are many private businesses which involve travel and longer work commitments as well as many workers moving to the cities for work perhaps while their partners remain back home. The opening up of the economy has meant that there are many who are opening up their own businesses. After living on a very small budget some people find they have a lot of money. Sometimes, the men will take a mistress, especially if they come to the city to trade for a while. When their wives find out they may seek a divorce.

Temptations are more common these days and people who are married today have many more opportunities to meet other people. A film director in India, himself divorced, said:

> There is too much pressure and temptation out there. It's going to become a nightmare. Every family worries. Is the

> man going to meet someone today? Or is he going to be seduced? Everyone lives in constant fear?

A man who works in a large company in Delhi started to have affairs after being married for three months:

> 'Indian men need other women', he says, 'adding that many of his friends also feel the same way. Family life is one thing, life outside is another. You don't have to hide it—everyone at work knows who my girlfriend is.'

You wonder whether the man's wife was aware of the affair and if she didn't how she would feel if she found out about it from a friend. The question also is whether this man would mind if his wife was having affairs also—do Indian woman need other men?

> Veena and Rakesh decided to have a marriage that left them both open to having affairs if they wished. They both enjoyed the freedom for a while until children started to come along. While Veena was stuck at home with the children, Rakesh was out having a great time with other women. When she started to object his reaction was one of anger, in that she was spoiling his freedom and treating him as though he was her property. They both agreed, for the sake of the children, that neither would object to the other having a fling. However, in Veena's case, as she began to age, less men became interested and those that were wanted only a secret affair so their wives did not find out. Rakesh had no such problem as he was in a very good job that carried power. For Veena a meaningful relationship both within her own marriage and outside of the marriage became impossible.

Other Indian women, who are aware of their husbands' affairs, refuse to have their own affairs as they believe that would make their husbands affairs okay and believe their children will respect them if they don't do such a thing. In other cases the woman sees preserving her dignity as the most important issue. While what I have written here seems to imply that Indian men are prone to having affairs, the situation is no different to the West where the majority of affairs are conducted by married men.

We can never be sure about these types of temptations unless we're faced with the temptation directly. And remember that food, drink and sex (to many people) are three of the most basic needs or wants that we face. That is one reason that people find it difficult to stick to diets, like fatty junk food and have affairs even if their relationship would appear to be happy. The above example I have given becomes a purely physical encounter. I hope that most people would find that a temptation like this does not meet with their needs as the real intimacy is at an entirely different level than you have with your partner. These needs should be met by our partner.

So we may think that we can be trusted but it comes down to our actions. And if we cannot trust ourselves on the smaller issues, such as promising ourselves to get fit or talk more with our partner, then often this lack of trust or commitment with ourselves is projected onto our partner—it's almost as if we are saying 'I can't trust myself so I can't trust you'. And a relationship will not survive if we cannot trust each other. We need to ask ourselves whether we would have an affair if there were no chance that we would be found out. And imagine if we did have an affair how we would face our partner, particularly in those intimate moments when the two of us are alone and we express to each other what our relationship means—I think it would be pretty hard and can be a reason why partners confess as the lie becomes difficult to live with. As society becomes more complicated there will be problems in a relationship, but it is important the couples enter a relationship with trust.

Communication on an intimate level will help to dispel any lack of trust. If we can trust our partner with our most intimate details or with a personal matter without fear of embarrassment or a feeling that they may criticise us then we are on our way to a trusting relationship. If we find it difficult to open up in this manner try some simple examples where we explain something that we have seen and describe how we feel about it. And not just 'I saw this old couple walking down the street...they would have been a least eighty years old...and they were holding hands'—we can tell our partner how that made us feel…'I think that's fantastic that people that age still do that sort of thing—it made me feel great...do you think we'll still be doing that when we're that old'. We're providing an observation about somebody else so if we're uncomfortable with this approach then it is not too personal, however we are able to then to talk about it and relate it to our own situation so we are including some intimacy and making it relevant to our own relationship. Introducing some humour will help to lighten the mood without taking away from the conversation.

Using this example, our observation of the older couple can then help us talk about what we will be doing as we grow old together—perhaps an overseas trip, spending more time with friends, taking up some hobby or sport. It makes it easier or a conversation to take place that is personal and relevant to our relationship. We can also learn to refer back to these conversations if we see something or someone that reminds us of what we had been talking about earlier. This makes it easier to keep the conversation in the relationship moving. Also referring back to an issue or subject that had been raised earlier that week by our partner indicates that we were listening and have an interest in what was said—this will help to avoid the attitude that 'I won't tell them about much because they don't listen anyway'. It will give confidence to our partner and help to keep our relationship healthy and exciting and our partner will continue to trust and confide in us.

We all have that feeling in our stomach when something doesn't feel quite right. We can learn to listen to those feelings and trust our judgement—they won't always be right but we are emotional people and therefore having a greater understanding of our emotions and feelings will count for much. Hopefully if we can show that we are trustworthy and that we do follow through with what we have committed ourselves to, then our partner will respond as well.

Values and Respect

The above two words are particularly important in a relationship. Values are what we believe—what we believe is right and wrong, what is important and what matters in our lives. Our basic values are often learnt from our parents either by being told at an early age, the difference between right and wrong or through example. Most of us are not aware of what our values are, but when asked we will generally come up with a list of things that are important to us, be it a stable family life, or honest friends, or a partner we can trust. We can also do this exercise with our own relationship by deciding what the important things in it are. By recognising our own values and how important they are, we are then in a better position to understand our partner's values and meet their needs on a daily basis. We should take the time to look at into what common values we may have in our relationship, and also any differences that there may be.

You should be able to see exactly how these values are of benefit to you and your partner and a reassurance from each other that they will be followed. These values can be as simple as respect and kindness; two words that help to build character and which mean that you have a concern for your partner. Our partner wants to feel important and noticed. For example, if they make an effort to look great then it is natural that they would like to hear how good they look. Bringing out the best in our partner will also bring out the best in us.

These values are important in our relationship with our partner and every effort should be made to practice these on a daily basis. As well as improving the relationship, having this common ground will assist if children are being raised, where we should be consistent in our actions.

Some values that we could consider in our relationship include:

- Being free to express our own ideas and thoughts—look to see if our relationship has one partner who tends to dominate or take over discussion, decision making and so on. A great relationship provides roles that are balanced, although one partner may be better or more interested for example in looking after the finances in the household. Putting yourself last and keeping your ideas quiet serves no purpose to yourself or your relationship. We should strive for equality in determining the important things in the relationship. In particular learn and apply negotiation and discussion skills so that disagreements are solved without moving into conflict or anger—listen to each other's ideas and thoughts and acknowledge and appreciate that they may be different. Hopefully our relationship allows mistakes to be made and is a tolerant household.

- Encourage learning and self-development in the relationship—having a partner for life does not mean that self-improvement is not relevant for either partner anymore. We need to encourage and be supportive of each other as we both pursue our interests and passions, both together or by ourselves.
- Base your relationship on love rather than fear or embarrassment. Many relationships are openly abusive, built on fear and involve violence. They are very destructive and if the partner is unwilling to change despite our best efforts then the relationship is best ended.
- We should look for a balanced relationship rather than one based on dependency, particularly emotional dependency. Some Indian women believe that it is important for a man to show his wife who is boss and that a woman is unable to choose her own friends. This dependency has often led to domestic violence. Some dependency is normal and healthy, however we need to learn to recognize any excessive dependency. Even though Indian women's status is improving and many couples now practice equality there will still be times where partners will struggle as they try and work out their roles in the relationship and how much influence they have with each other.
- Dependent people often express jealousy and control their partner, to the extent of viewing other people as a threat to the relationship. A dependent relationship

can cause one partner to have limited personal growth and a lack of interaction with other people. As India becomes more open there are greater opportunities for everyone to try new experiences and these should not be restricted within the relationship. If one partner is dependent on the other we can try the following:

- Discuss what each of us wants out of the relationship—why are we together and what do we want out of the relationship.
- We should look at fulfilling our own responsibilities, rather than relying on our partner—a certain amount of independence in the relationship is fine.
- We can create a greater sense of independence within our partner by encouraging their self-development, needs and dreams.
- We can improve our own self-respect by following some of the examples in this book.
- We learn to trust our partner.

- We should be supportive of each other. This can apply to a range of situations such as when one partner is ill, under stress at work, or having family problems. In a relationship with children it is important that each partner support each other on issues where any children are present—disagree out of their sight, but come back to them with your decision with both partners agreeing. A show of intimacy in times of stress will go a long way to relieving any pain, even if the problem doesn't disappear overnight. This could be as simple as a hug or kiss, a note left on the kitchen side, or a word telling them how we feel about them. It is very important that one partner should not feel like they are having to face problems alone.
- We need to respect each other by focussing on each other's strengths or good points, not weaknesses or shortcomings. We'll have a far more positive relationship as a result. One partner may be better at organising, so the general running of the household,

such as paying the bills could be their duty. We all have our weaknesses—it is far better to focus on our own weaknesses and try and fix them up rather than looking at our partner's weaknesses. We can also cover for each other's weaknesses. If you do not think your partner is competent then you will not ask for their assistance when needed and then they will not seek your assistance for fear of being laughed at by you. We need to learn to have faith in our partner and let them know from time to time that we do respect their value. Our partner can bring a different view to issues that can help our own ability to make a better choice on things.

- While we do not always agree with each others' point of view or a decision that has been made, we respect the choice each other has made and respect each others' right to think and choose. It could be as simple as deciding what to do on the weekend. Learn to speak up and express your views—in a relationship we need to have the confidence that our partner will listen to us.
- In respecting our partner's ability to make a decision, it is important that encouragement is also given if our partner is undertaking a new venture, whether it be a university course, business or a general interest activity. With the greater opportunities now available in India, many people are looking for new adventures and ways of improving themselves. It could be very disappointing to have a partner who says 'Why would you want to do that' or 'you always start something but never finish it' instead of 'sounds great, tell me all about it'. Having a partner who has this positive attitude is helpful for people who tend not to finish what they start—encouragement and support goes a long way as a means of indicating that our partner believes in us and what we are trying to achieve. A negative comment or lack of support can put our partner off from undertaking something—we need to encourage our

partner even if they decide to stop doing what they set out to do. We all make mistakes (and making mistakes is the best way to learn) and it is at this point that you should be able to count on support from your partner:

- We are only too happy to support our children in their activities so there should be no reason not to support and respect our partner in what they want to do. We should learn to appreciate what these interests mean to our partner and be enthusiastic for them.

- Respect for our partner also means knowing when and how to assist. If it's a project or task that is close to our partner's heart (perhaps a hobby or a new skill they are learning) then they may want to do it by themselves. There's not a problem in wanting to help, however we need to find out whether our partner actually wants assistance. If we're not sure then we should ask in such a way that they have the option to refuse our help in a nice way. For example, 'that looks interesting (or you're doing a great job with that), would you like some help', rather than 'I'd like to help you with that'. And if help is required then assist them happily—there is nothing more annoying than someone coming in with his or her thoughts and then taking over or making nasty remarks.

I have mentioned the word respect a number of times above. As children we've been told many times to respect our elders. We do this in a number of ways including listening to their advice, being patient if they happen to be slow, tolerating any strange behaviour and watching our manners around them. The family has always been particularly important in India. One's first duty is to the welfare of one's family and working family members often would put their financial resources together. Respect for elders has always been a large part of Indian family life, particularly in the rural villages. It has been quite common for a number of generations to live under the same roof.

We treat the older people that way because we accept them the way they are. We actually show them respect, rather than just feeling or thinking it. There is no reason then why our partner should be treated any differently and that respect should be visible. Little things such as interrupting when our partner is speaking and putting each other down in front of other people are quite significant habits that indicate a lack of respect and are embarrassing. We need to think about what we are going to say, particularly if it involves criticism of our partner as it is difficult to respond to in front of other people.

> 'My husband likes to point out my faults in front of his friends and work colleagues when we are out', says Sanjana. 'I cannot say anything as I may embarrass him and then he will say something when we get home. I ask him not to do it but he thinks it is funny.'

While we shouldn't take ourselves too seriously, embarrassing our partner can over time start to affect their confidence and offering the excuse 'I'm only joking, don't take things so seriously' doesn't make our partner feel any better.

I praise Wendy in public—learn to praise your partner in public and in the privacy of your home. We should not tell everyone how good our partner is and then when we get home turn it around and abuse them. There will be many things we liked about our partner when we got married. No matter how angry we may be or however stale our relationship may feel, the chances are our partner still has these likable qualities. We need to regularly tell our partner what we like about him/her. When our partner is reminded of their attractive qualities, they tend to respond with warmth, gratitude and affection. I know it works with Wendy and I, so give it a try.

Respect for our partner also flows from self-respect—that is, liking ourselves for who we are and not for what we can or cannot do. If we do not like or have a reasonable opinion of ourselves then it can be difficult to have a close personal relationship with someone else.

We are all capable of making changes for the better to ourselves if there is enough motivation or inspiration to do it. A lack of self-respect may lead to one partner having affairs, an over-dependence on pornography or a lack of interest in their health and general appearance, even though they genuinely love their partner. If we are aware of any hurt that may result from our actions, we should change our behaviour to stop this from happening. We should accept all responsibility for what we are doing and where our actions are taking us and our partner.

Problem Solving

Indian society, in this modern day, still emphasises sharing values and having harmony and devotion to the family. However, as pointed out in this book this sometimes comes into conflict with the pressure to pursue education and jobs that may take a family member away from the rest of the family or the need to work extra hours. These conflicts only become bigger problems when couples avoid open communication with each other that will lead to disagreements. Avoiding this direct communication with each other will increase the risk of relationship problems particularly if couples attempt to keep outward harmony while having unresolved issues within the relationship.

Any negotiation or problem solving in a relationship should have the following characteristics:

- Appreciation—we should feel appreciated by our partner. We need to listen to what our partner is saying and be positive in any comments or reaction to what is being said. Sometimes repeating the point being made by our partner indicates we are listening, and gives us a chance to clarify any misunderstandings. We should offer our partner an opportunity to put their side of the story, or their ideas.
- Welcomed—we should feel we are an important part of the relationship. One sided discussions on an issue usually indicates one partner wishes to dominate and decide on an issue and the other partner's views are not welcome.
- Trusted—we should feel as though we are trusted by our partner. As I have previously outlined, trust is extremely important in a relationship. By allowing our

partner the opportunity to express an opinion shows that we trust their judgement.

- Recognised—our thoughts and ideas are important, and mean something to our partner. We should not listen, and then simply dismiss our partners thoughts and ideas. Both partners in a relationship will have different viewpoints that are worth listening to and considered. The knowledge that our partner will listen and consider our ideas will encourage open and fruitful discussion, leading to better problem solving and decision-making.
- Decision making—both partners should feel as though they can make a decision. If one partner tends to make the decisions most of the time, the other partner will not speak up and offer an opinion. Both partners should have an equal ability to make important decisions, or at least be included in the decision-making process. This is especially important where a decision involves the family as a whole and everyone is affected by what has been decided. Harmony within the relationship and family becomes easier and the flow of ideas becomes easier and fun.

Couples need to have discussion on such things as recreation choice, religions, friends and their goals in life. Some of these issues are quite important to the relationship as they involve day-to-day issues. In discussing any problems or issues within a relationship the following are some suggestions that may assist:

- Both partners should identify what the problem is—it is important that the problem itself be identified, rather than blaming the other partner for mistakes.
- Look at possible solutions to the problem. This means listening to each others suggestions and not dismissing them as no good—consider all possible solutions by having an open mind.
- Look at the good and bad sides of each possible solution to the problem so you eventually both agree with a possible solution. However, both partners

should be positive as optimism helps to solve problems, whereas anger may encourage one of the partners in the relationship to walk away before an issue is solved. Positive emotions will help to build trust in our relationship. I have spoken about emotional maturity earlier in this book.

- Both partners agree to a possible solution and try this solution to see if it works. This allows the partners to work as a team in carrying out the solution. Agree that if the solution does not work then the problem can be looked at again.

As we take greater control of what we really want, we can determine and improve our character and future as well as assisting our partner to do the same—we can start working as a team. We are then moving towards a more balanced relationship.

Balancing Your Lifestyle

8

This book so far has looked at things that will hopefully provide you with a more balanced relationship—a relationship that will make and keep you both happy. We all have different demands in our lives these days and finding our priorities in life is not easy. Often we lead lives that are anything but our own, particularly when we consider our work, friends, relatives and so on.

You may have heard the word 'globalisation' and it is a term used most commonly for the joining of national economic systems through international trade. India and other countries such as China are good examples of countries that have opened up and become world economic superpowers. It can also mean social, cultural and technological exchanges have become world-wide. This globalisation can also be seen in some of the other issues that have been discussed in this book. There is a world-wide trend towards obesity, lifestyle diseases such as diabetes, increasing household debt, an increasing number of women working full time, increasing divorce rates and an ageing population. It shows, quite alarmingly, how trends, good and bad, are common around the world.

Here in Australia, a recent discussion paper written by the Australian Federal Sex Discrimination Commission titled, *Striking the Balance—Women, Men, Work and Family* examined the role of men and women in Australian society with respect to the sharing of household chores and paid work. The paper said that the current common arrangement where women do most of the housework and child-care and men were the main breadwinners worked against 'the principles of a democratic and just society'. The paper believes that the unequal division of work between partners threatened health, family relationships, workforce participation rates, women's retirement income and fertility rates, particularly if women carried the major responsibilities for children and ageing relatives—the paper pointed out that women are the main carers for elderly relatives. This can increase women's chances of poverty in old age (particularly if they were divorced).

The paper saw men as also being disadvantaged in that they have less opportunity to form that close relationship with their partner and children—They have 'overwhelming financial responsibility for family, insufficient breaks from work and insufficient time for family and intimate relationships'.

And as the population is ageing there may also be a case for men to take greater responsibility for caring for ageing relatives.

The change in today's society—including high divorce and separation rates, more single parent families, increasing work force participation by women and the conflict between career/ home, ageing population and greater household debt—has meant that certain changes outside the household are required to allow greater flexibility (such as family-friendly work places). Now, many young Indian people want to embrace Western lifestyle even further, but in a social structure that is largely not prepared to support them.

A work-life balance, or having good control over one's working conditions and personal life, has become more important for India to overcome a population that is ageing while also being able to maintain its international competitiveness. It's not an easy task to balance the need to maintain your income as well as having that life outside of work that includes the importance of maintaining a great relationship with your partner. It is a struggle that most people face everyday and sometimes that control is taken away from us if the culture of the work place is towards work first and family second.

As I have mentioned earlier, females in India are looking more towards having a satisfying career and this includes the ability to compete with men where necessary. In addition encouraging and examining more efficient ways of working which does not necessarily mean measuring how long you work, may also hold a possible solution to the falling birth rate and some of the other problems in relationships.

The above changes affect each relationship to a different amount and therefore each relationship needs to examine ways that best suit their circumstances.

As mentioned earlier relationships can be similar to running a business; a home business. There is a need to consider financial planning, care of the home, child-care, shopping and many other tasks. And this does not even consider our social or personal needs.

For us to focus on any one area in particular over other demands can lead to resentment and relationship breakdown—for example, some people see their career as more important than family life. In other cases we concentrate on the smaller issues and details of our lives that we cannot see the important ones—today's urgent tasks tend to take over our lives. It is therefore important that our relationship examines what the important aspects are and every effort is made to follow these. Aspects of our lives to consider include our own relationship, immediate family, career and social/leisure. Within each of these there will be other things to consider that will also compete for our time and energy and are worthy of consideration.

As earlier mentioned relationship and family living has changed over the past twenty years in India. People are working longer hours and there always appears to be less time in the day to do things. Those with children are running from one activity to the next. Any free time is often a time for recovery only rather than a time for undertaking some real leisure, having some fun or catching up with friends. Basically our lives can feel as though they are out of balance, we feel frustrated and our enthusiasm and energy levels are low. A life that is in some sort of balance provides the energy and enthusiasm that helps further achievements.

While suggesting a more proactive lifestyle so that we can gain a greater control over what happens to us, I am not suggesting that we try and fit in as much as possible so that we almost run from one thing to the next. There have been a few books that suggest that we as a society and as individuals, should be slowing down, perhaps in some way to make up for the speed of change that has been occurring last century and this century and a more highly stressed society where time and keeping busy is seen as important. So we can look at setting our own pace where possible; a pace that we're comfortable with and provides us with the opportunity to take on what we really want and which fits into our relationship.

As humans we are also social people and most of us feel far more purposeful when we participate in useful and interesting activities and spend our time with other people. For many of us a major part of this participation occurs during the week involving our work as well as other activities and we look forward to the weekend to rest and recover. However, if for example our weekends tend to come and go and we don't do much and perhaps it feels a little empty then it can make us feel isolated from other people and perhaps even depressed. This situation can be as depressing as when we have a lot of demands placed on us.

Despite our complaints that our lives may be directed by others (for example, in our work place) and we are always following a routine, sometimes we feel safer and emotionally healthy with some structure that makes us work and interact with other people and a sudden but regular change from this situation can be uncomfortable—particularly if the lack of participation in things or isolation is regular rather than just occasionally. The loneliness that we may feel as a result can affect our relationship, particularly if only one partner is affected by this lack of participation. I used the example earlier in the book about the husband who stays at home and watches television all the time. Imagine if his wife would like to do things such as going for walks or visiting friends and he just wants to sit there doing nothing. This type of relationship soon becomes boring and can quickly lead to such dissatisfaction that one partner will seek excitement elsewhere. I will talk later in this chapter about how to go about being more proactive in your life.

The Need for Money

As the world becomes more commercial and competitive, people in countries such as India where the changes have been the greatest start to take a real interest in what money can buy. Not that long ago basic subsidence was the main concern of many citizens—while it was a struggle people could rely on others and life was a lot simpler. Now in India more people are spending their money on housing, cars, medical and health care, entertainment, leisure and tourism. Today people are buying their own homes through housing loans at the banks. The number of people in India who have their own homes has greatly increased. Leisure goods such as wide screen televisions and labour saving devices such as the latest washing machine and fridge are becoming increasingly common. Travel overseas by Indian people is increasing. While many in India are concerned about the obsession with money, most see this as a side-effect of the booming economy and prefer it to the older situation.

However, if we're not careful our lives become more concerned with having the latest wide screen or plasma television, the latest computer or the most up to date mobile phone than maintaining good relationships. Our society almost expects us to have the best and to get these at any cost. We're not seen as successful unless we have the latest or the best job and many of us are caught in the trap of setting a standard that often requires both partners to work (and often with children who still need looking after which falls to after school care or elderly parents). Many people are concerned with how materialistic society has now become and the pressure on relationships that this presents, particularly husbands who have to find the income. How often do we go looking for a bigger home or apartment and better car and then turn around and take them for granted and want to move onto something even better. The more things we like to collect, the more we go looking for more in order to try and maintain the level of happiness that these things supposedly bring us. And if our friends and relatives are also spending a lot of money or have the capacity to spend more money than us on themselves, then we can feel poor if we don't at least try and match what they are spending. Of course we all need to plan for retirement and planning financially is a worthwhile cause and should not be ignored. It also allows us to lead a reasonable lifestyle and enjoy what life can provide, but we need to be wary that it does not take all our time and effort, or be seen as the source of contentment and happiness in our lives.

Economic success has not necessarily produced a comparable standard of living or sense of contentment. An overemphasis on working life and long hours of work have made it difficult for many Indians to enjoy, or to participate actively in their own family's life and the life of their community.

We should look at our relationship and see if it is dominated by the need to spend money, to have the best. If so does it make us anxious, unhappy or give us a feeling of being unsuccessful. Sometimes, we have the feeling that we will never be satisfied now matter how much money we have.

> "I'm not looking for an economic supporter but an emotional partner", says Indira, a 32-year-old office worker.

When I talk to people it is as though many are striving for the excesses in life—the excess mortgage, the newer, better car. People's live are often driven by the advertisements they see on television and the marketing of the latest gadget or product. I know home loans in England, Australia and the US (and elsewhere) are now taking up a bigger proportion of people's incomes than ever before.

However, it makes it difficult in a society that is driven by the human need to spend and the need to keep up with everyone else, when people struggle because they do not earn so much money yet they feel an obligation to compete. Sometimes, we are driven by our children's wants as they often desire the latest and it has to be brand names. The availability of easy credit and ability of people to be able to place everything on credit makes it easy to over-extend.

Most of us have probably 'invested' in the lottery in the hope of becoming rich overnight. Very few achieve that wealth but even fewer stop to wonder what would happen to them if they actually won. We believe that we will be able to handle the instant wealth we don't have even though most of us are only used to living on the average wage.

A man in America became one of the biggest lottery winners in history a couple of years ago. Since his winnings his marriage has broken up, he has had a drinking problem and family associated with the man have also started to have problems. The level of happiness or unhappiness of lottery winners generally only lasts a short while. Research undertaken by the University of Illinois compared the happiness level of the very wealthy in America with those of the Masai herdsmen of east Africa—it did not find any difference in the levels of happiness between the Masai and the very wealthy. Wealth therefore does always mean happiness.

At the relationship level this need for the material things in life can mean we are only interested in our own self-interest and what will bring us instant, but not long lasting, happiness. We can certainly enjoy the financial rewards resulting from our work and any investments. We should not try to put so much pressure on ourselves and our partner in trying to earn that extra the dollar. We need to look at ways to reduce our spending by keeping things simpler—look for things we need, rather than what we want. We have probably all thought about what we would like to do after we become rich. However, for most of us the level of wealth we would like may not occur so perhaps it is better to start to find a way to do those things you would really like to do but just in a smaller way.

So instead of trying to get those possessions and money at this very moment we should be looking at doing what we really want to be doing at this very moment.

If we have or wish to pursue a hobby or interest then this is often an area where we need to be spending some time so that you are living and enjoying the present rather than wishing for something better at a later stage. A hobby or interest is an area where you can spend some of the spare dollars you may have—it is not then a case of trying to spend our money so that everything we have is the latest and the biggest. For example, if you enjoy photography then look at purchasing a good camera and perhaps equipment to develop the photos so that you can do everything yourself. Similarly, you may enjoy the outdoors (camping, hiking, or perhaps would like to give mountain bike riding a go) but never seem to be prepared or have the right equipment to take advantage of the weather and the great areas that may be close by. If you are committed to becoming fitter then spend some money to attend a nice gym or buy some exercise equipment for the home.

We'll get a greater sense of achievement from providing for these things than buying the latest computer because our current one happens to be two years old and everyone else has the bigger screen. We should be a bit more careful in our spending habits, so that it what we want and not what our materialistic society sees as acceptable and we can focus on our life and the direction that it is heading and not what other people are doing with theirs. Change has to start somewhere if we want to move away from the need to consume so we can live our own lives and improve our relationships.

How to be Proactive to Establish the Balance in Our Lives

In many situations we do have choices in our lives and it can be case of whether we exercise these choices and perhaps do things differently, or continue to live our lives the way they are now. This statement is important if we are not happy where we are at this moment. If problems and issues, particularly those that we don't seem to have any control over, tend to dominate our lives, we need to try and develop a more proactive approach rather than a reactive one, so that we do have more control. This type of lifestyle also means we have a greater opportunity to do what we want to do and be what we want to be. It can also mean stepping back and looking as to whether our life is currently overloaded or just out of balance.

If our lives do feel out of balance or lack some purpose, then we don't have much choice but to look at ways where we can become more fully involved and in control of our lives. The only thing that is stopping this happening is ourselves and in most cases it involves knowing that changes are required as well as a change of attitude. In leading a more proactive lifestyle then we can consider the following:

- Make a commitment to a lifestyle that emphasises proactive living—we can see ourselves doing what we want to do and living a life that more closely reflects our interests. We can commit to a lifestyle that will keep us enthusiastic and more fully occupied than we may be at this stage. This of course does not mean ignore the responsibilities that form an important and necessary part of life and our relationship. Some commitments such as children's activities and taking care of aged relatives will come first, but if a more proactive approach is undertaken generally, these real commitments may not appear so hard and we may even be able to bring some new energy and enthusiasm to them as we can see there is more balance in our lives.
- We can take a look at where we are at the moment, our commitments, the type of lifestyle we and our partner lead, and where our life may be out of balance. We may feel that we are fully committed at this point of time with things such as work and family, but there may be other things we'd like to be doing. We could think of instances where we would have liked to have undertaken something, whether it was a one-off situation liking seeing a friend or a longer term commitment such as undertaking a course at a university, but our current life did not allow it or there were obstacles in place. Thinking about it now could we have managed to fit in what we really wanted to do—if so, we can remember that lesson next time...if not, how can we make it work in the future, perhaps by moving a few commitments around (remembering our desire to take more control), or speaking with our partner about any compromises that may be required—

'I'd love to do this course, but it's run on a Tuesday night when our daughter has her piano lesson—is it possible for you to be at home so that you can pick her up for the next three months while I do my course?' Look for solutions that can help both of you, rather than anything that may stop you doing what you really want to do.

- In looking at our current lifestyle we can see if there were times when we were proactive, how it felt (good or bad) and why we felt that way—did we have to delay the housework or ask our partner to do it? Was is doing something for ourselves that gave us the most satisfaction (taking the initiative), or the actual experience whether it be learning a new skill or helping somebody out—it doesn't really matter as long as you felt good about it. Wendy started up a home delivery cooking business with a girlfriend. They loved cooking but running a business was the exciting (and scary) part. They learnt a great deal in the way of running a business and had to suit their cooking to a commercial market and there was an excitement in doing something for themselves and having that control. The business gave them the confidence and they were doing something for themselves.
- We can look at our priorities in life so that we have a better chance of achieving the balance we are seeking. In terms of relationships and family it often comes down to high priority being given to appointments that have to be kept, jobs that need to be done at home, or relatives to visit.

Those urgent tasks will take care of themselves and generally have to be done. However, in considering the other things that need to be done, we can perhaps look at the value or interest that these matters hold for us. In this we can write a list if necessary of both the urgent/routine matters that require doing and matters that we consider will be worthwhile, perhaps fun, doing. This can be done on a weekly basis and we make sure that we do include tasks or matters that mean something to us—the activities that feel good which may include spending more time with our partner in taking walks, playing a game or just talking, doing some exercise or reading that book we've been meaning to start. As each week goes by these types of activities should start to become a habit. Self-education is a great way to break any monotony or routine that we can all slip into. I have thoroughly enjoyed undertaking a number of short courses—the course work itself, the people I have met and the general feeling that I am not too old to learn something new. Choosing something we know we will enjoy is important otherwise our efforts will be wasted.

I set priorities for keeping fit. I generally know from week to week when I will exercise—nothing will stop me exercising, although I am flexible if necessary. Wendy and I make sure we have fun with our children as it has value for both them and us. So we try and stay focussed and perhaps set some goals, otherwise little things may distract us and we will end up with the 'I haven't got the time' excuse. And when we become involved in a task, an activity or simply watching television, we should focus on it and learn to give it a 100%. We are the fully attentive mother/father when we are interacting with our children—they are very smart and will know when our attention or interest is not fully with them. We are the attentive partner who listens closely, shows interest and focusses fully on what our partner is saying.

Goal Setting

We need goals to determine what is important and what isn't in life, motivating us to achieve and building confidence as we reach or exceed these goals. These goals can help provide us with priorities to follow. Set goals which are achievable, but we also may need to change these goals as we work through them. It would be safe to say that our general goals will fall into all or some of the following:

- Family and home;
- Financial/career;
- Physical and Health;

- Spiritual;
- Social;
- Mental and education.

In setting goals we can perhaps look towards Kaizen, a Japanese method of production excellence and industrial efficiency which began during the 1930s and 1940s. Kaizen is a method for creating quality products efficiently through many small and continuous changes.

To start our own personal Kaizen, we can sit down and make a list of things we would like to improve and then think of changes to help achieve this improvement. We then look at ways we can improve in that area such as 'how do I free up my time so that I can get more exercise or spend more time with my children, or what small change can I make that will improve my relationship'. With these small changes we can remove the fear that a large change is required to start our improvement. We have to be comfortable with these changes so that any fear we may have will disappear.

We then move on from this to make this habit a continual one so that we are always looking for small but steady improvements. We can then imagine the changes we can make to our lives if we continue to make changes each week for the rest of our lives. Try the following:

- Do away with having fixed ideas—free your mind to other possibilities.
- Think of how to do something and not why it cannot be done.
- Learn to not make excuses by looking at what you are currently doing that is stopping you improving or stopping you achieving something you really want.
- Do not seek look for perfection, even if it means that you do not reach your goal or target straight away. Do it right away even if it feels uncomfortable.
- If you do make a mistake or failed to achieve what you really wanted then, correct it right away or look at where you can achieve it next time. Ask yourself 'why'

and seek the causes of where you may not have achieved.

- Seek the advice and experience of other people rather than trying to go it alone.

The following will also help us in our goal setting:

- Setting goals that we really want to achieve or want is important, not something that we have just because we should have something to look forward to. For example, we may have some financial goals, but we try and avoid pursuing those at the expense of our own personal relationship or relationships with other people. In setting goals it is important that we look at goals that are going to provide us with the most happiness in the present rather than what may make us happy in the future. By looking too much into the future we can end up not enjoying ourselves in the present. I also touch on this later.
- We need to be aware that our sub-conscious often rules the way we behave. Most people cannot concentrate for more than a few minutes on activities—our concentration wanes, we think on other things, we go back to what we were doing but often have lost what we were concentrating on. We need to set our goals in writing and then place these into our sub-conscious.
- Be realistic—we don't set such high expectations that it will be near impossible to reach, leading to a 'well I did try' response. However, we should also strive to achieve the best so that there is a real sense of achievement in reaching the goal we have set. Perhaps we can look at something we can measure such as increasing the distance we can walk in half an hour, over say a two-week period if we are looking at getting fit. We make the effort and enjoy the experience as it happens, but even if we don't quite make that distance we were trying for, we will have gained some increase in fitness level.

- I have already touched on the benefits of focussing on being positive rather than being negative. While we can look to see where we want to go in our life, look at how you can change anything in the present moment.
- We write our goals down and review them often, particularly if we have a habit of not completing our tasks or goals. In setting goals we need to actually see our goal, as visualising our goal will make them realistic and more visible. If the goal is to spend more hours with our partner or family then we detail how we will achieve this. We look at both our week and the week of our partner (and children), particularly where there are commitments. There may be some free time (or find some time) and decide that you will take the kids at that time to kick the football, fly a kite or bike riding. We should never underestimate the importance of play with our partner and our children. Apart from being fun, it can be surprising how much more we may learn about other people in a play situation than in conversation—play with our children has also given us the opportunity to find out what happened at school that day, find out whether there are any problems and teach them about sharing, fair play and so on. They will sometimes be more inclined to open up in a more relaxed, perhaps fun, atmosphere or in a situation where there is movement.
- Most of us have a goal, or would like to have more money either for luxuries such as a holiday or for when we get older and have retired from work. We can have a plan and write down how we might achieve this through extra savings, improving our education so we get a better paying job and so on. And look at having this exciting future by creating something now.
- We really need to be honest in our assessment of what we need to improve, or turn our mind to in order to both set goals and achieve them. They could be issues that we have thought about for a little while but not got around to it. Many Indians will now see some of

their fellow country people earning good money and having a much improved lifestyle. Perhaps you can examine and understand how some of them have become successful—how have they done it, what sacrifices have they undertaken to achieve their goals. Be proactive and undertake your own self-examination. Share your assessment of yourself with your partner so you have someone who can assist you and provide feedback on what you are thinking. It could also be a shared assessment process so that you inspire each other to improve.

- We should never be afraid to try new things. Making a list of things that will inspire us and provide us with a new experience is the first step. It could be many smaller experiences such as visiting somewhere or someone different every weekend. We may even pick a talent or passion for something that we didn't realise we had such as playing a musical instrument. These experiences, if undertaken with our partner, will also bring us closer. I believe that the more 'roles' we fill, the more sources for improving self-respect we have and the more interesting we become. In looking for new experiences we need to be careful not to overload ourselves—activities that we enjoy should not be rushed or undertaken when we happen to have a spare moment. We should plan for them so that both us and our partner are aware of that commitment to ourselves and then we won't feel guilty.

There are many books written about the problems that the modern day woman faces—attempting to have the career, the loving partner, the children, the nice home. It could be someone in their twenties or thirties who has a career but also wishes to have children but does not want to give up her career. Because of rapid economic advancement in India the focus has often been on these women who now have the opportunity to be more financially independent but who are now realising that it is not that easy to achieve all they want to. Often these women are frustrated, angry and sad who feel it is near impossible to have it all. In some cases these women may have executive jobs, but are single and feel like they are a failure because they have not been chosen by someone to spend the rest of their lives together. In other cases women feel that there are so many choices and satisfaction is important, that they feel trapped.

Also unless compatibility between work and family life is improved, the trend toward later marriage, no marriage and fewer children will not stop. It is important for us to have access to many options so that we can choose the path we want to take. However, the current situation in India is such that the freedom to choose is limited and the balance between work and life is becoming more difficult. Society needs to make it possible for people to work more flexibly.

In other cases there has been a feeling in India that 'what Indian women fear most is being identified as female'. This is said because every woman is trying to prove that they are equal to men, as Indian society recognises and tries to enforce the equality between men and women. This sense of equality among urban women has resulted in more marital conflict in family life as many men have not been taught or recognise that women are equal to them.

In trying to prove that they are men's equal, women will sometimes loose their own female identity. Also, as I have pointed out earlier in the book, women can still be burdened with the heavy work in life so there is no real balance in their life. In many cases both men and women felt that a successful marriage depends on a woman's ability to make the adjustments necessary as the marriage moves through various phases and to provide the stability—*Women are like roots, men are like trees. Only if the roots are there, the tree can stand.*

Some solutions, in the work place, to what many see as a modern day problem have been implemented in the West and will become more common in India. There are many work places that do offer assistance for working mothers either through more flexible work hours, child minding at work or the opportunity to work from home. There are more opportunities these days for women to undertake paid work in India—it is more acceptable and the workplace will become more work/family oriented. However, there will always be people out there who will miss out or struggle to find new roles in a changing society. Perhaps they need to start looking at their relationship and how it can support the choices that women (and men) want to make. We'd all like to have the ideal well-paid job, ideal partner and well-behaved children. It doesn't always work that way. However, as one woman from a rural area says:

> 'It is only my own self-confidence, ingenuity and industriousness that will help to make me happy and prosperous and gain equal status with men.'

And a quote from an urban woman:

> 'I am now encouraged to study and work harder and to develop as a new type of woman, with strong morals, a good level of education and a strong sense of discipline and a high self-esteem, self-confidence, self-reliance and self-strengthening.'

While India maintains a traditional economic system and a male-dominant society and women are expected to stay home and take care of their families despite the level of a woman's education, ability, or career hopes, Indian women have begun to take a more active part in the business world. Entrepreneurship rather than employment in large companies is one area where Indian women perhaps have a greater opportunity of advancing in their careers.

This is partly driven by a desire for independence, flexibility, and a need for personal fulfilment. As noted earlier, Indian women are becoming more career conscious and in some respects this will enable them to become more financially independent. While some headway has been made in terms of making the work place more female friendly it would appear that one way that the Indian woman can move ahead is to become more entrepreneurial. And the Indian woman, like women of other societies, has an advantage for a number of reasons including their understanding of consumer spending as they are the largest consumers in India (particularly if they undertake the budgeting in the household), they are more use to juggling a number of tasks at once, particularly if they do have a career as well as a family and they have little obligation to give their family financial support as this is undertaken by the husband. There would appear less risk for them to start some enterprise themselves as they are not the principle money earner.

It is difficult to offer solutions to every situation and the issue of the modern woman in particular as just described can be real, however those two quotes indicate that the Indian women have the strength and confidence to improve themselves.

The increased opportunity for women to pursue their careers and have fulfilling lives outside of marriage is important to understand. In the past marriage was the only choice for women. However, as women's employment opportunities have increased, they have become more independent economically and are in no particular hurry to marry. Many are hesitant to marry if they must give up more promising career chances and the opportunities that greater financial rewards brings. In this respect it is important that for relationships to survive each couple must look at their own circumstances and decide if their current lifestyle is helping or working against their relationship.

I have mentioned in this book that one of the most important factors affecting marital satisfaction is valuable time spent together—the way married couples spend their time at home.

This could be as simple as housework and childrearing, hobbies, recreation and sports on holidays, dining and relaxing on weekends. Consider these as valuable time spent with your partner. Relationship problems will often increase after the birth of the first child because of the huge emotional strain on the wife, who in a nuclear family must face childrearing practice without husband's support. In order to reduce the burden of childrearing experiences it is important for the fathers to be encouraged to perhaps take child-care leave, to come home earlier from work and, importantly for married couples, to share more home activities. I enjoyed helping around the house when our three children came along—I felt included (particularly as a new child can take all the attention in the family) and an important part of the family. It also greatly helped Wendy as she was feeding the babies at night and not getting a lot of sleep.

The following are some suggestions in trying to find a better balance:

- Look for certain types of work or careers that are more family friendly—ones that offer more flexibility in terms of hours and time off.

    A teleworker has two daughters aged 3 and 7. At the moment she usually works at home every Wednesday, saving a long round trip to her work in central Delhi. For the rest of the week, she has flexible working hours, leaving the office at 4 p.m. and resuming work at home from 8 to 9 p.m. after collecting her children from the day-care centre.

- Consider setting up a business that can be worked from home—office work from home is becoming easier with computers and e-mails. Technological advances now allow women to utilize the Internet and their computer skills to manage both career and family. Small offices/home offices are becoming more popular in India and from a society point of view is becoming more acceptable for woman to work this way.
- As mentioned in an earlier chapter, if there is that struggle at home to find time to do everything such as child-care, leisure, fitness and health, financial management and general home care, then it is important that the family sit down and work out an agreeable/ workable program.
- Try and balance the four major aspects of your life—family, money, work and time.
- Workout what the important and not so important tasks are within each of these.

Hopefully some of the guidance in this book will also help both men and women to achieve a better life balance. This can only help improve a relationship.

In trying to balance our lives we will often examine where we are at in our lives at this present moment, what we have achieved and 'what is my purpose in life'. Sometimes, we can appear lost and as though we are looking for something. Some of us will say that it is to worship our God and undertake his wishes on earth. Others see making money as a lifetime ambition and will often lead an unbalanced life to achieve this objective. However, many people reaching this goal realise that there is more to life than just making money. They forgot about relationships and forgot about living, in trying to create their 'perfect' lifestyle.

We should see life as a series of experiences and adventures, great and small. Experiences could be career, children, family, friends, travel, hobbies, study, entertainment, etc. We can enjoy each of these experiences within our relationship. We can enjoy one day at a time by looking at our achievements (and listening to our partner's) for today—did we learn something, what was good or enjoyable about it, did we make a difference, however slight, to someone's day and did we make the effort to compliment or praise our partner? We should live in the present—when we think of the past we start to despair and perhaps think of our mistakes, lost opportunities or regrets and when we think about the future we often become anxious, disillusioned or just unsure of what we are going to do. Living in the present gives us more control, helps us to be more focussed and inspires us to live the moment. But that does not mean we do not plan for the future and have those goals I mentioned earlier.

We can therefore start by enjoying our experiences as they happen and we may be surprised that our future will become what we want it to be. Try and make it happen right now and enjoy the journey. We can do the things we enjoy whether it be exercising, reading, undertaking a course, or spending more time with our partner.

Through these experiences we can make a contribution both to our own lives and also to others around us. We can take a look at our partner's contributions and acknowledge the good things they are doing and we should tell them that—they will enjoy the compliment from you and also the fact that you have noticed what they are doing. It can be as simple as saying how good the house looks after they have cleaned it, a compliment about a good dinner, or the contribution they are making to the business.

In moving towards a more balanced life we should avoid going looking for perfection in ourselves or others. We tend to worry if our children don't come up to expectation, whether it is on the sporting field or in the classroom. Does it really matter if they don't score near the top of the class—'Reena did better than you—why can't you achieve the same?' There may be an obsession with grades, colleges and doing well to the extent that parents have forgotten about good behaviour, modesty and politeness, particularly as society becomes more competitive. We generally would like a return to the times where people were perhaps kinder to each other. In our relationship we need to forget about being competitive with our partner. We should see our relationship as a team where we both have common goals and these goals are achieved together and in harmony with each other. Any mistakes made or problems to be solved are for the team to address, not one partner in the relationship.

We can all be pretty hard on ourselves (and our partners in some cases) at times, particularly when we, or our partner, do the stupid things or make a mistake. Think about when you may have acted too quickly without thinking or made that mistake and ended up looking a bit silly or felt that you had let someone down. It's probably easy to laugh about it now, however at the time we probably got angry with ourselves, or our partner. We can acknowledge where we may have gone wrong, learnt from it and then we can move on. We look for a better balance, where our mood most of the time is one of being positive. Our positive nature will be reflected in our relationship as we inspire those around us.

In our relationships or our job, not every day is going to go according to plan—something or someone is likely to come along and do its or their best to try and ruin it for us and we need to accept that within life not everything will go as we have planned. Our lives will never be perfectly balanced but we can go looking for simple solutions to try and iron out any problems that we may face. We need to learn to be flexible in moving towards this balance.

Being aware that priorities will alter through the life of our relationship is important and in some circumstances a concentration in one area may be required in the short-term (for example, if and when children come along, our priorities will change and our time will be taken up by the new baby), however if both partners acknowledge the important parts of both the relationship and life in general then the relationship has a much better chance of surviving and getting better over time.

Nothing in this book will work for our relationship unless we make an effort to make changes and adjustments where required. We make our commitment and then try our best to follow it through. Taking small steps may make us feel more comfortable and is a good way to start. India has been going through some large changes and this has affected the people of the country. I have mentioned some of these changes in this book. These changes have happened quickly and people will always struggle where there are fast and big changes. These changes have meant greater freedom and more opportunities for people to better themselves. Relationships will also improve as people can marry for love rather than arrangement and there is more equality between men and women.

As your confidence grows you will find that moving into any new experiences is both natural and exciting—look forward to discovering new experiences and new ways of approaching your relationship and with it the opportunity of something great. It is important that you note any changes and how it has affected your outlook on life...and don't forget, take your partner on this new journey.

A little girl once said, 'How wonderful is it that nobody need wait a single moment before starting to improve the world.'

I wish you all the best and hope that you find a new happiness in your relationship with your partner. It is the most important part of your life.

Appendices

APPENDIX 1—STRENGTH TRAINING

Why don't people strength train?

Only a small percentage of people undertake a regular strength training program and experience and observations lead me to the conclusion that a lot of the training is not effective or appropriate (in terms of time and results) and in some cases can lead to injury. Consequently, an ineffective and time consuming programme often results in the programme being abandoned and you will often find that people will never go back.

Other reasons include not understanding the importance or implications of strength training (and hence no desire), a misunderstanding, particularly by women, that lifting weights will lead to big, unsightly muscles, the general lethargy in the community towards exercise and not wishing to set foot inside a gym.

Training Specifics

A note of caution before commencing. While the following programme is very simple and is explained in detail, there is no substitute for hands-on instruction. Therefore, if you have not undertaken a strength training programme before, it is strongly advised that expert assistance is enlisted to help you begin the programme. You should be able to comfortably perform the basics before being confident enough to continue on your own. As you work through his programme you will see some great results over a two to three month period, particularly if you have not exercised this way before. Following that you may find that your results plateau to the point that you are not making the gains that you had experienced at the outset. That is normal as the incremental gains will gradually reduce to the point where no further gains are possible—be comfortable with that. I have included some variations that will test your body every so often that will help you maintain both your interest and the gains you have made to date as well as assisting in making small incremental gains.

While it is recommended that this strength training programme be undertaken only once a week, it is safe for beginners to train twice a week with light weights while learning technique—you will not overtrain and it will fast track your development. Once you are comfortable with your lifting and can lift progressively heavier weights with confidence then reduce your training back to once a week.

In undertaking the exercises, the following should be followed:

- All sessions should commence with a light warm-up (exercise bike or light jogging for example), joint rotation and finish your workout with a good stretching session.
- When lifting any weight keep your back in its neutral or natural position that you have when you are standing with good posture. That is, with the slight hollow that we all have, so you don't hump or arch your back. Follow the 'brace and hollow' procedure—that is, tighten your stomach (as when you cough), then pull it in and hold it in place as you go through the exercise movement. This is important as it stabilises your whole lower back area.
- Generally only one set of about 10-12 repetitions maximum is undertaken preceeded by a warm-up set of 5-10 reps using about 50% of the weight to be lifted in the main set. 5-8 reps only using heavier weights can be undertaken for the main set to really enhance muscle growth, but should only be done when the exercise movements have been mastered.

At the end of the set there is momentary muscular failure (i.e. it is very difficult to complete the last repetition, but make sure you can rack or rest the weights or have someone there to assist).

- For those not used to lifting weights, it is not recommended that you train to this point or lift heavy weights until you have become confident with the movement and can fully control the weight you are lifting—this may take a number of weeks, but progressively increase the weight by small amounts or numbers of repetitions each, or every few, training session. Those new to strength training should lift only light weights initially until the exercise can be performed competently.
- Weight train in this manner only once a week.
- Undertake the squat, leg press or lunge before any upper body exercise as they are the most taxing of the exercises prescribed and therefore should be undertaken first.
- Warm-up before undertaking the session and cool down after the weight session to reduce possible soreness.
- Ensure that you undertake the above weight training when you are freshest, so that maximum gains are achieved and there is less likelihood of injury.
- Have a 2-week break from the weights every couple of months to rest your body.
- Allow about 2 seconds to lift the weight and 4 seconds to lower the weight and do so in a smooth action without jerking the weight.

Exercises

The exercises below are the sum total of what a good full body strength workout requires. They are not all required to be undertaken in the one workout and as such I have included a sample programme at the end of this section. I have also indicated the major muscles that are affected by the exercises.

The Squat

Position yourself under the bar, placing the bar on your trapezius muscles (triangular muscles near your neck). Squeeze

your shoulders together. Have your feet about shoulder width and slowly squat. Your buttocks move out first as you begin to squat, so that your back remains in the neutral or natural position throughout the exercise—do not hump or arch your back. Your knees should not move further out than your toes. As your quads reach parallel to the ground (do not go any further) slowly press the weight up pushing with your hips. This exercise in particular needs to be performed extremely carefully, because of the weight sitting across your shoulders causing downward pressure on your spine. I would suggest that if you have a back injury or any stability problem to perform the lunge or leg press only—2 seconds up and 4 seconds down.

The Lunge

Position your feet about a shoulder width apart, with your feet pointing straight ahead. Step forward with one leg keeping your forward leg centred over your ankle. Make sure your knee does not go beyond your toes. Slowly bend the back leg and

drop slowly down, keeping your back in its neutral, or natural position. Focus on your front leg. Your stance does not need to be too long as this strains the quads in the back leg—2 seconds up and 4 seconds down.

Leg Press

You will find the leg press machine in most gyms and I recommend the one where you sit and have to push the plate on

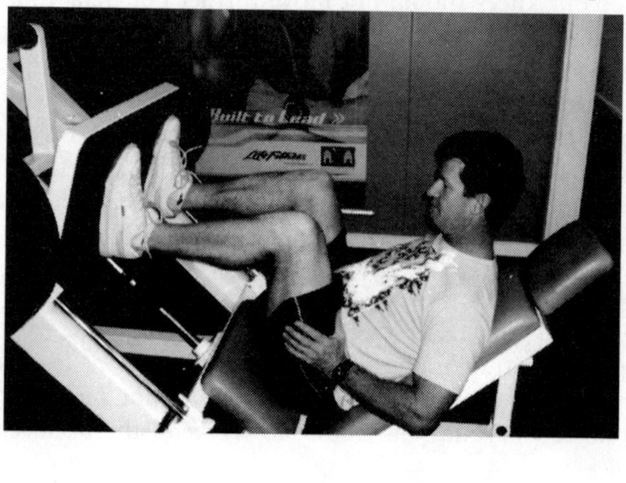

a 45 degree angle away from you rather than the machine where you push your legs straight forward. Sit with your feet flat on the plate. Release the weight and slowly bring your knees towards your chest. Do not bring your knees right to your chest as you will put pressure on your lower back. Hold for a moment and then push slowly up until your legs are almost locked—2 seconds up and 4 seconds down.

Dumbbell Flys/Bench Press

Sit down at the end of the bench with the dumbbells on your thighs. Lie down keeping the dumbbells close to your chest. Keep your hips and shoulders on the bench and feet on the floor. Push the weights straight up and make sure your shoulders are back. Imagine you have an egg siting on your chest—you will trace this outline. Slowly lower the dumbells, tracing the egg shape as you lower them. The dumbbells should

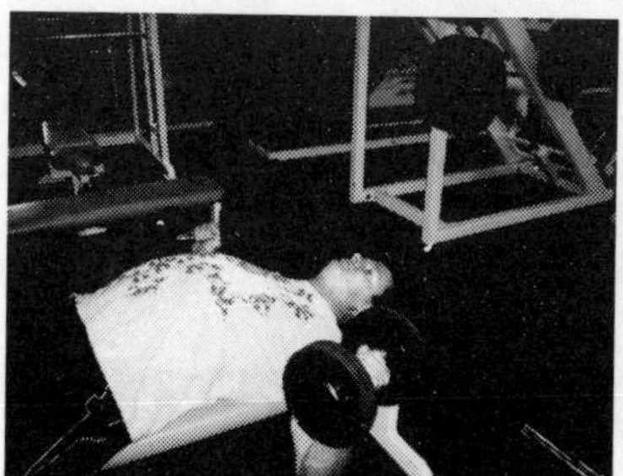

be even with the bench and no further down. Slowly raise the weights tracing the egg once again. Your back should remain in a neutral or its natural position throughout the exercise. You can also try the bench press with the dumbbells—instead of taking them in the egg shape take the dumbbells straight up and then down, about shoulder width apart. In both exercises do not take the weights below shoulder level—2 seconds up and 4 seconds down.

Barbell Bench Press

Lie down on the bench, feet flat on the floor. Keep your hips and shoulders on the bench. Use about a shoulder width grip. Lower the weight slowly all the way down to a point just below

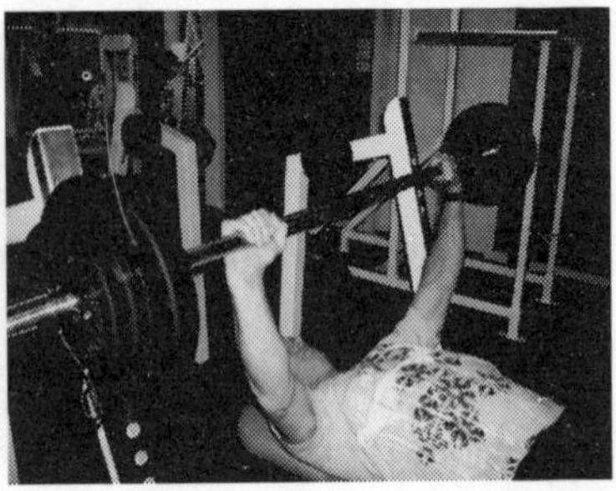

the nipples. Pause and then drive the weight up with your elbows almost locked. Lower the bar and repeat. Your back should remain in its neutral or natural position throughout the exercise—2 seconds up and 4 seconds down.

Dumbbell Row

Place one knee on the weight bench, with the dumbbell weight on the bench and start with your lifting arm straight. Keep your body straight and parallel to the ground. Focus on raising your elbow as you raise the weight. Pull the dumbbell into your hip, while keeping your elbow tight into your body, then slowly lower without dropping your shoulder—2 seconds up and 4 seconds down.

Lat Pull-down

Sit with feet on the ground. Reach up with your palms facing you and grab the bar about shoulder width or slightly narrower. From this stretched position pull down the bar to your chest while contracting your back muscles. Keep your elbows close to your body, your chest high and your abs and

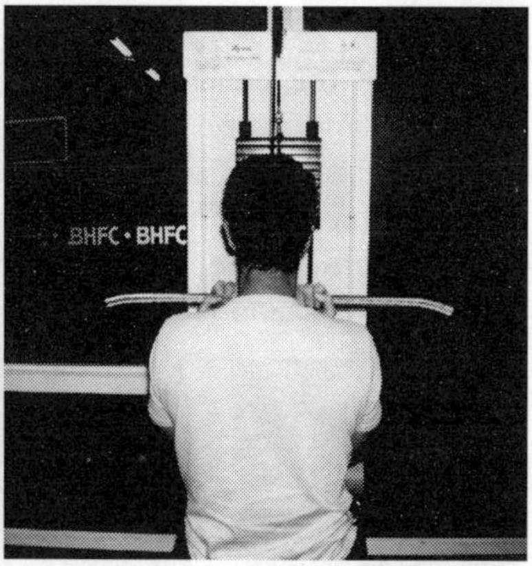

lower back tight. Let the weight up slowly until your arms are almost fully extended—2 seconds down and 4 seconds up.

Chin-up

Grasp the bar with your fingers pointed towards you, hands about 10 inches apart. From an extended arms position pull yourself up high until your elbows are close to your ribs. Bring your face next to the bar, not under it. Lower yourself slowly—2 seconds up and 4 seconds down.

Seated Cable Row

Sit on the bench with your back in neutral or its natural position and knees slightly bent. Your arms will be fully extended and lean forward to get a good stretch. Pull the handle to your waist, keeping your elbows close to your body. Squeeze your shoulder blades together before returning to the starting position—2 seconds towards you and 4 seconds away.

Sample Programme

Week 1	Week 2
1. Leg press/Squat	1. Squat or lunge
2. Bench press or Flys	2. Bench press
3. Lat pull-down	3. Lat pull-down
4. Up-right row	4. Chin-ups
Week 3	**Week 4**
1. Squat or lunges	1. Squat/leg press
2. Seated or up-right row	2. Seated or up-right row
3. Bench press	3. Lat pull-down
4. Chin-ups or lat pull-down	4. Bench press

Programme Design—Summary and Variations

In implementing the above programme the following parameters are provided as a quick easy to refer to guide. As mentioned some flexibility in this programme is appropriate to offset boredom and the variety will encourage growth and progression:

- Speed of movement: 2 seconds lifting/4 seconds lowering.
- Exercise order: legs first, then upper body.
- Amount of work: 4-5 exercises per session for upper and lower body.
- Frequency: twice a week for beginners, reducing to once per week for the experienced.
- Intensity: lighter weights/more repetitions for beginners, increasing to heavier weight/less repetitions for the experienced.
- Recovery: rest between different exercises of between 1 and 3 minutes.
- Repetition: One warm up set and then heavy set, 8-10 reps for each—heavier weights and less reps for the experienced and lighter weights and more reps for the beginner.

The following alternative sequences can be used every so often to prevent boredom and assist in muscle strength and growth. These should be undertaken once you have a good understanding and technique with the basics:

- 10-15 reps of maximum weight, then drop 20% off weight and do another 10-15 reps and then drop another 20% off weight for 10-15 reps (3 sets max.)—best with a partner so the weight can be dropped quickly, or have the other weights ready.
- With the bench press, get someone to help you lift the weight up (you will be lifting a greater weight than you normally do) and then you bring the weight down slowly (about 2 seconds up and 4 seconds down). The eccentric, or lowering, is where the strength and size is gained most (the pec muscle is being stretched).

- Do two sets of different exercises for the same body part, for example, dumbbell fly and then bench press (about 2 minutes apart or straight after each other).
- Do 2-3 reps of very heavy weight, have a break for up to a minute and then do another 2-3 reps—continue until you can't go any further.
- Start with light weights and build up to heavy weights (do max. 20 reps only each time).
- Have very little break between each different set, to get an aerobic work out as well.
- Alternate between upper and lower body in the work out to give each a rest.

As an additional variation try experimenting with your strength-training programme by including some body weight exercises. This will capture both your strength and cardio training programme in one hit as well as providing a little more intensity to your training. For example:

- Complete a warm up set of bench presses or flys and then your heavier set and then do as many push ups (on your knees if necessary) as you can and then back to a lighter bench press or flys and then back to push ups and then back to a heavy set. Do this until it becomes difficult to perform your usual number of push-ups. As an example, following a heavy set of the bench press (5-7 reps), I'll do thirty push-ups. Following my second set of bench presses, I might manage twenty-five good push-ups. I've usually had enough when I can perform ten push-ups, with the last two or so a real effort.
- Perform a set of upright rows, seated rows or lat pull-downs and then try some chin-ups. Go back and forth as per the example with the bench press. These exercises will work primarily the biceps, triceps and lats.
- Perform some lunges, squats or leg presses and then hop on an exercise or road bike for a minute or so

(you judge the intensity based on your fitness level but try a reasonable pace) and then go back to the leg exercises. Repeat as many times as possible.

- As a variation to the above, try the bench press or flys and then do some chin-ups and with the rows or lat pull downs compliment them with the push-ups. The weight training exercises are using different muscle groups to the body weight exercises so that you can push out more with each exercise. You will notice the difference between this method and the first three.

Many people find the chin-up difficult to do—persevere with it, but if after a time it still can't be done concentrate on the push-ups and leg work. Push-ups can be done either on the knees or with the full body off the ground—if you can only manage the former work towards getting your body off the ground.

The above don't need to be done every week as they are quite tiring and you may have some muscle soreness the next day, but it is a simple yet fantastic full body exercise programme. Performed quickly but carefully the above three examples could be covered in around ten to fifteen minutes, which is great if you are time pressed. It also enhances our strength endurance capacity (any activity that requires using a reasonable amount of strength or effort for an extended time), so that a brisk walk up the hill or an extended period working in the garden poses no problem at all. Your recovery rate from these other activities will also be a lot faster.

APPENDIX 2—READER FEEDBACK

Dear Reader

This is Book 1 of a two-book series. This first book outlines my experiences in a great relationship and how it could be applied to a relationship in the changing, more westernised Indian society. I propose to write a second book which will include more personal experiences of Indian people within their own relationship, and how they deal with conflict and other issues arising out of their relationship.

I need your help in putting this second book together. I would love to hear your story and experiences so I am able to provide even more knowledge to the Indian people. In order to help, I have included some questions below which provide a focus on the issues I am interested in addressing, and also to provide feedback on this first book. If you have a story outside of these questions, please feel free to include them.

- *Do think this book will help in your relationship and what else could I have included?*
- *Is your current relationship (and previous ones) happy, intimate, abusive etc?*
- *How could your relationship be improved—for example, sharing of duties, equality, communication?*
- *If you could, would you leave your current relationship?*
- *Have you had, or thought about, an affair while in your current relationship?*
- *For you, what are the most important components of a relationship?*
- *How do you deal with conflict in your relationship?*

Your story and experiences can be emailed to me at the address below (please, no more than one to two pages). In the interests of your privacy, I will not reply to your email. All information provided will be kept private and confidential, and fictitious names only will be used in the second book.

I look forward to hearing from you. I wish you well.

Best regards

Geoff

wherridge@westnet.com.au